'This book is an invaluable and long overd
history of Black feminist activism in the UK. B
interviews and poetry from members of Man
Women's Cooperative, and analysing contemp
Black women, their families and communities, it is a timely and necessary
contribution to the UK's Black feminist archive.'

Shirley Anne Tate, Associate Professor in Race and Culture, and Director, Centre for Ethnicity and Racism Studies, University of Leeds

'This book has made visible the often hidden history of Black women's activism and grassroots organizing against injustice and oppression. It offers detailed and grounded testimonies from Black women involved in a range of struggles, and brings together gender politics and anti-racism activism to deepen our understandings of the key role that they have played, and continue to play, in shaping the history of Black people in Britain. This is an inspiring, powerful and uplifting book that pays tribute to the courage and strength of Black women, and is a welcome addition to the literature on Black people's historical legacies.'

Professor Claudia Bernard, Goldsmiths, University of London

'*Catching Hell and Doing Well* is a praisesong for the women who founded, organized, and developed the Abasindi Women's Cooperative. It is also a coherent and forceful critique of a society and economic system that seek to undermine Black lives and deny our self-actualization. Diana Watts and Adele Jones have cogently shown how the Abasindi women employed the personal and political in a radical liberatory stance. They also reveal the similarity of Black experience in White-dominated societies in terms of economic disadvantage, the racialization of poverty, the alarming drop-out rate of Black high school students, the criminalization of young Black men, and the incarceration of Black children in foster care. *Catching Hell and Doing Well* thus has an international appeal, and can be used in comparative studies of the Black experience. This book is powerful. I wholeheartedly recommend it.'

Afua Cooper, James Robinson Johnston Endowed Chair in Black Canadian Studies, Dalhousie University

Catching Hell and Doing Well

Catching Hell and Doing Well
Black women in the UK –
the Abasindi Cooperative

Diana Watt and Adele D. Jones

A Trentham Book
Institute of Education Press

First published in 2015 by the UCL Institute of Education Press, University College London, 20 Bedford Way, London WC1H 0AL

ioepress.co.uk

© Copyright Diana Watt and Adele D. Jones 2015

British Library Cataloguing in Publication Data:
A catalogue record for this publication is available from the British Library

ISBNs
978-1-85856-671-9 (paperback)
978-1-85856-672-6 (PDF eBook)
978-1-85856-673-3 (ePub eBook)
978-1-85856-674-0 (Kindle eBook)

All rights reserved. No part of this publication may be reproduced, stored in a retrieval system, or transmitted in any form or by any means, electronic, mechanical, photocopying, recording or otherwise, without the prior permission of the copyright owner.

Every effort has been made to trace copyright holders and to obtain their permission for the use of copyright material. The publisher apologizes for any errors or omissions and would be grateful if notified of any corrections that should be incorporated in future reprints or editions of this book.

The opinions expressed in this publication are those of the author and do not necessarily reflect the views of the UCL Institute of Education, University College London.

Typeset by Quadrant Infotech (India) Pvt Ltd
Printed by CPI Group (UK) Ltd, Croydon, CR0 4YY
Cover and title page: photograph of Paula Jones

Contents

Acknowledgements	viii
About the authors	ix
1 Abasindi Black Women's Cooperative	1
2 The legacy of Black women's activism	11
3 Cultural expressions of resilience	32
4 Ancestral journeys and diasporic connections	58
5 Loving body, skin and hair	85
6 Sowing seeds of success	109
7 The politics of sisterhood	130
8 Reflections	158
References	164
Index	177

Acknowledgements

Although this book was written by the two authors named on the front cover, it represents a collective endeavour of the women of the Abasindi Black Women's Cooperative. Not only have we drawn on archive material and the memories of Abasindi members, family and friends, we have been gifted with photographs, interviews and poetry that have brought the book to life. But beyond publication, there is no debt of gratitude to repay because each contribution reflects an individual commitment to see the work and achievements of this vital organization documented for posterity – sisters and brothers, we hope we have done you proud. Alongside our historical analysis, we have woven in discussion of some of the contemporary issues affecting Black women and their families and it is clear that racial and gender equality are still distant goals. Additionally, the current political and economic climate has set back many of the gains of Black and working-class communities and it is our hope that this book will inspire the new generation of activists.

We acknowledge the women of Abasindi, past and present, and the friends and family members who have contributed to the material for this book; please accept our apologies if we have overlooked you: Nkosi, Dkizo, Yinka, Zinzi, Thembi, Ashley, Abubakarr, Paul, Olajomke, Melanie, Yvonne, SuAndi, Shirley May, Kath, Abina, Pauline, Shirley, Abiola, Miselo, Moiwale, Kaya, Liz, Francia, Magdalene, Joy, Evadney, Lorraine, Tara, Sam, Caroline, Maria, Louise, Esther, Chalana, Patricia, Emense, Mumba, Estree, Gina, Lorna, Alima, Malaika, Norma, Paula, Beverley, Doreen, Mary Murphy, Deene, Mama Elouise Edwards, Mama Lindiwe Tsele, Mama Cynthia Gordon, Mama Julie Asumu, Dudu, Popgee, Doretta, Coco, Rose, Mary, Sibongeli, Betty, Pat, Amina, Barbara, Madge, Charmaine, Merle, Bernadette, Tinu, Christine, Tina, Sandra, Laverne, Sharon, Brenda, Talla, Viveen, Saidat, Ruffina, Dorothy, Carol, Luna, Veronica, Ruth, Marcia, Judy, Ken, Alti, Conway, Jedi and Yvonne Ahime, Mohammed, Andrea, Dorett.

ABASINDI CO-OPERATIVE

'SI ZALELWE UKUSINDA'
We Were Born to Survive

About the authors

Diana Watt is Senior Lecturer in Youth and Community Work Studies at Manchester Metropolitan University and an Associate Lecturer with the Open University. Her PhD research was on three generations of mothering practices among Jamaican heritage women in the UK. Over the years, Diana's political work with Abasindi Black Women's Cooperative has inspired her personal and professional development in the field of education and community activism. She was one of the UK researchers on the National Teaching Fellowship Learning and Teaching Research Project entitled *Diversity and Achievement: How non-traditional students succeed in higher education* and together with colleagues she has completed the research on *Promoting Cohesion, Challenging Expectations: Educating the teachers of tomorrow for race equality and diversity in 21st century schools*. Her publications include book chapters and essays on mentoring and the early development of youth work in the Black community, and she is also one of the trustees of the Louise Da-Cocodia Education Trust.

Adele Jones is Professor of Social Work at the University of Huddersfield. With a long history in social work practice and academia (including six years at the University of the West Indies), she specializes in international children's rights and is the author of numerous publications on various issues affecting children worldwide: child abuse, residential care, migration, child refugees, gender and the impact on children and families of HIV-AIDS. Her most recent publications arise from UNICEF-commissioned research she undertook on child sexual abuse in six Eastern Caribbean countries, which led to a three-volume series of books on the topic, published by Palgrave Macmillan: *Understanding Child Sexual Abuse: Perspectives from the Caribbean* (2013), *An Integrated Systems Approach to Policy and Programming for Preventing Child Sexual Abuse in the Caribbean* (2014) and *Cross-Cultural Practice for Addressing Child Sexual Abuse in Clinical and Group Settings: Lessons from the Caribbean* (forthcoming).

Chapter 1
Abasindi Black Women's Cooperative

The Moss Side People's Centre – Abasindi Co-operative

Introduction

> When we speak we are afraid our voices
> will not be heard and when we don't speak
> we are still afraid, so we might as well speak.
> (Audre Lorde, 1995)

The name Abasindi – the Zulu word for 'Survivors' – was chosen by members of the organization as a tribute to the strength, resilience and competence of Black women, in particular those in Africa and the African Diaspora that were actively involved in struggles against the dehumanizing and oppressive forces of apartheid, neocolonialism, racism and sexism. This book provides a historical account of the birth of Abasindi Black Women's Cooperative and traces its political impact as a significant contributor and historical antecedent to the social movements that tackle race, class and gender oppression in the UK. In documenting the work and achievements of a community organization that warrants a place in history, the book connects the reader to the resurgence in feminist scholarship and the role of Black women in present-day community activism. Though it is primarily the work of the two named authors, the book draws on the contributions and recollections of many Black women who were involved with Abasindi – 'we move with memories':

> We move with memories
> Voices we remember
> In places we no longer recognise
> Like tides they wash over us
> So that if we stand perfectly still
> Possibly, we can hear the sea.
>
> The benchmarks of our journeys
> Are not measured by distance
> But by the rubble of demolition
> As society moves on
> We just grow older.
>
> Our every days of normality
> To work, school, the market
> Are made from homes
> Distanced by thousands of miles
> From this place we reside
> So that we recognise fellow passengers
> As the strangers we see daily.
>
> Old people
> Who once danced on their toes
> To rhapsodies of yesterday
> Now move
> Pass symbols of their longevity
> As their feet tap a nervousness to arrive
> And return home.
>
> This is a place for moving and waiting
> Day dreaming, wondering to go or to leave
> Smiles are wide to faces seen for the first time
> And secrets are carelessly leaked to people
> Who may never meet again.

Abasindi Black Women's Cooperative

Cafe culture is held fast
By the grease of English breakfast
Served all day
As kitchen gossip turns a nosey eye
To a single lady sipping tea
Society has changed
But morals are still fashioned
As in the old days.

How many kisses welcomed
Those waiting on those to arrive
And their departures damp with sadness
Their ghosts
Are still visible in names of sweethearts
Penknifed into metal
And the angst of love discarded
Wept its agony into wooden post scars.

Yellow caps parading workmen
Interrupt
The daydreams
Swinging a sledgehammer of time
Drilling away the past.

Close your eyes
To hear the wild scream of a child's excitement
For adventure
Compete with the shriek of brakes burning rubber
As a choir of voices rise together
Typical, either there are none
Or they all come together
As heads in military precision
Nod towards the empty dock
Going, going, gone.
('We Move with Memories', SuAndi © 2014)

SuAndi, Abasindi woman, is a freelance poet and writer and was the Director of the Black Arts Alliance, one of the most important Black networks in the UK. She has produced three anthologies of poetry and for more than 20 years has written, performed and conducted workshops at community events in Manchester, and across the UK, Europe and the US; her poems appear in several poetry collections and her work is featured in gender and writing courses. Her numerous works include a monodrama, *The Story of M*, and a libretto for the

SuAndi

opera *Mary Seacole*. Her critical engagement with the representation and aesthetics of Black British writing has earned her international recognition especially in relation to women and race, and she is a long-standing guest poet for the British Council Writers Tour. An unsung heroine of Black British culture SuAndi's poetry has inspired many people. A multi-talented artist and performer, her work is underpinned by her unshakeable ideals as a human rights cultural activist and campaigner against racial inequality. The poems that feature in this book have been dedicated by SuAndi to the memory of the Abasindi Black Women's Cooperative.

The aims and objectives of the cooperative were to provide a social support base for Black women, a community resource centre and supplementary and cultural educational facilities for Black children and young people.

Over time, this concept was stretched to encompass men who shared the aspirational goals of the cooperative and the gains and costs to women's personal and political lives of adopting a position that questioned the very basis of White, western feminism. Through the use of research, archive materials, narrative interviews, photographs and poems the social issues that inspired their action for change are explored. Clarke (2003) argues that in celebrating the achievements of women in the past, we also need to acknowledge and challenge the problems that women are faced with today.

As members of Abasindi, the authors are following in the tradition of many Black women writers who invoke their own concrete experiences and those of other Black women whom Omalade (1994) refers to as Griot-historians. Omalade argued that the role of the Black woman Griot is unlike that of the historical role played by male Griot in West African societies. She further argued that before a language that captures the experiences of Black women in the Diaspora can be created, the Griot-historian must break 'de chains' and become submerged in the waters of Black women's pain, power and potential (Omalade, 1994: 105–6). However, Collins (1990: 15) points out that scholarly work of this nature is generally not attributed to Black women artists and political activists, hence the creation of a 'false dichotomy between scholarship and activism, between thinking and doing'. This book is therefore aimed at bridging the gap between scholarship and activism in respect of Black women's political struggles within a historical and contemporary context. In drawing on their personal and professional perspectives, which are grounded in over two decades of community activism and scholarly reflections, the authors weave together the story of Abasindi Cooperative and in so doing reveal narratives of political struggle that have their resonance in present-day society.

Over the years the membership of the organization consisted of women, the majority of whom were the daughters and granddaughters of immigrants from Ghana, Sierra Leone, Nigeria and the Caribbean islands: Trinidad, Aruba, Barbados, Jamaica, Grenada and Saint Kitts. In Manchester some of these early migrants were among those who were involved in the establishment of the West Indian Overseas Coordinating Committee (WIOCC), the West Indian Sports and Social Club, Westwood Street in Moss Side, Cariocca Enterprise and the Arawak-Walton Housing Association. The idea for the Moss Side Arts Group was rooted in the rich tradition of Black culture and creativity that existed in Manchester from the days of post-war Caribbean migration.

Many of these men and women arrived at a time when England was regarded as the 'mother' country. In his poems 'Me Ago England' and

'Culture', J.D. Douglas (1985) writes of the immigrant's expectation of benefiting from this relationship. Sam Selvon's novel *The Lonely Londoners* (1956), however, deals with the shattering of the illusion of belonging. Unlike other immigrant groups, the West Indian was seen as failing to conform to the expectations of English society. The Cypriots, Maltese and Italians were often held to infringe criteria of neatness and quietness but most were thought to live respectable family lives. After earlier experiences of signs that stated 'No Irish, No Blacks, No Dogs' or 'No Poles, Eastern Europeans or Jews,' Polish people eventually gained respect as conformist and solid householders keen to improve the state of their properties. On the other hand, people from Southern Ireland were often said to be 'as bad as the darkies' (Patterson, 1965: 178–9).

Black sexuality was viewed as a threat to White femininity as in the *Daily Mirror* article entitled 'Introducing to you ... the boys from Jamaica – Are they stealing our women?' The *Mirror* went on to reassure its readers that the arrival of Black women would now ensure that Jamaican men did not steal 'our women' (Webster, 1998: 60). This article on the 'boys' was the only reference to women and represented a shift away from the 1940s view of Black women.

However, up until the 1960s the literature on migration focused primarily on the experiences of men. Although women were totally absent from Lawrence's (1974) study on *Black Migrants: White Natives*, it was nevertheless described as a study of 'Race Relations in Nottingham'. Pryce (1979: 300) justified the exclusion of women from his study on *West Indian life-styles* because of the limitations of his research methodology. He stated that 'as a male researcher, I had only limited access to women in the West Indian community for research purposes'. Morokvasic (1983: 16) drew attention to the representation of female migrants as 'an accessory of a process they are not really taking part in'. In her studies on women's experiences of migration Pedraza (1991: 304) points out that 'we have yet to develop a truly gendered understanding of the causes, processes and consequences of migration'.

Both Lawrence and Pryce failed to make reference to the activism of Claudia Jones, whose membership of the Communist Party led to her arrest, imprisonment and subsequent deportation from the USA to Britain in 1955 (Sherwood, 1999). Claudia was born in Trinidad and had spent much of her formative years in America. Within three years of arriving in England she was responsible for the launch of Britain's first post-war Black newspaper, *The West Indian Gazette*. Claudia Jones later described the *Gazette* as having served 'as a catalyst, quickening the awareness socially and politically of

West Indians and Afro-Asians in Britain for peace and friendship between all Commonwealth and world peoples' (Sherwood, 1999: 147).

Donald Hinds, who worked on this paper alongside Claudia Jones and was among London's first Black bus conductors, noted that the *West Indian Gazette* came out at a time when 'White passengers would bounce straight up out of their seats if a Black ('coloured') passenger was bold enough to sit next to them'. Some of the White passengers would rub their hands on the 'coloured' bus conductor's hair for luck. Hinds reported that following the explosion of racial disturbances in April 1958, Claudia was among a small group of people that went on to organize the first indoor carnival, which was held at the St Pancras Hall on 31 January 1959. Prior to the Notting Hill Carnival, which first took to the streets in the late 1960s, six indoor carnivals were held at different venues in London between 1959 and 1964 (Hinds, 2008).

During this period immigration was a key issue, and one of the effects of the 1962 Commonwealth Immigration Act was the splitting up of families. This was particularly the case with older children, who the state did not consider to be dependents. In response, Claudia Jones was one of the community leaders who organized a mass demonstration against this Act (Carter, 1986). Her death in 1964 marked the beginning of collective action on the part of Black women against racism, poor working conditions and sexual discrimination within the workplace. African-Caribbean women workers were at the forefront of the 1971 night cleaners' strike for better working conditions (Bryan *et al.*, 1985).

In the light of these experiences, this book represents an acknowledgement and celebration of the activism and achievements of the daughters of 'ordinary women' who came together individually and collectively and achieved 'extraordinary' things. It also represents tales of hope, solidarity, cooperation and the triumph of community spirit. Every woman who was a part of Abasindi reflected these principles but there was one woman who embodied them all: the late Kath Locke, one of the organization's founders. Shirley May, in a poem dedicated to Kath Locke, refers to Abasindi women as 'the jet-Black fabulous jazz of isosceles'. This reflects a politics of sisterhood bound by a commitment to race and gender equality within an everyday context which, though future-oriented, was informed by the past:

> Tomorrow
> We stand in all our yesterdays,
> Where the valiant had once stood.

Where heroes now stand
For we have come too far
So we battle like
Queens should.
Mothers called to combat,
Like the battalions of our families,
All those who did not lie down
Whilst others took possession
Of our rise and fall.
Spirited like our mother's mother
And our mother's before
We did not yield ground,
But braced ourselves for the journey
In hulls of tall ships to distant shores.
Bejewelled cargo of victors and brave women
We are the jet-Black fabulous jazz of isosceles,
We stand in all our yesterdays
Where the valiant had once stood
Where heroes now stand,
You set a path for us to ascend
To find the very best in us,
As we enter the city gates,
We are people that have battled,
Against those who would try to defeat us.
You made us strong, you gave us your voice
You left us with your songs, told us to rise,
On the dawn, and to overstand the storms,
You made us spirited,
We are Kenya, Egypt,
Senegal, Rwanda,
Mali, Libya,
Madagascar, Nigeria,
Jamaica, Barbados, we are Trinidad
We are a people called to arms,
A people not afraid.
We are the jet-Black fabulous jazz of isosceles.

('Kath Locke', Shirley May © 2014)

Abasindi Black Women's Cooperative

Kath Locke

Summary of the rest of the book

Chapter 2, 'Legacy of Black women's activism', sets out the social and political context that gave rise to the Abasindi Cooperative based on the experiences of women from the 1960s onwards and reflecting a continuation of Black women's activism in the work of Una Marson and Amy Jacques Garvey. It describes the specific ways in which Black women seized freedom and thus gained the power to act and the freedom to grow as a collective. Through the use of research, archive materials, narrative interviews, photographs and poems the social issues that inspired their action for change are explored.

Chapter 3, 'Cultural expressions of resilience', explores the involvement of Abasindi Women's Cooperative in the promotion of African-Caribbean art forms as part of a broader struggle for recognition and representation. Additionally, it examines the strategic relationship of Abasindi with other organizations sharing similar goals; for example, the organization's link to the development of the Nia Centre, the first 'cultural' space in the North-West to focus explicitly on African and Caribbean art forms. These forms of cultural activities were in fact building on the work of the West Indian Overseas Coordinating Committee (WIOCC) and the Roots Festival.

Chapter 4, 'Ancestral journeys and diasporic connections', discusses the work of Abasindi Drumming and Dance Group in enabling Black women and young people to rediscover the value of their own culture within the African Diaspora. It was also an opportunity to develop the creativity of its members. The role of music, dance and other forms of creative expression as a central function of community life is also explored.

Chapter 5, 'Loving body, skin and hair' deals with these sites for broader political struggle among Black women concerned with race and representation. The chapter also discusses the ways in which Black haircare and skincare became a focus of challenge to the racism of cultural neglect within a care system that distorted Black children's self-image and damaged their self-esteem. This chapter documents the importance of loving the (Black) self as integral to positive identity formation, and at the political level calls for an acknowledgement of cultural diversity and respect for difference in meeting the needs of children in care.

Chapter 6, 'Sowing seeds of success', discusses the emergence of Black supplementary schools in response to Coard's report: *How the West Indian Child is made Educationally Sub-normal in the British Education System* (1971). It goes on to look at the role of Black women in the development of Abasindi Saturday Supplementary School and that of the Louise Da-Cocodia Education Trust, which was established in 2008.

Chapter 7, 'The politics of sisterhood', is an acknowledgement of the ways in which Abasindi created its own version of feminism, crossing boundaries and building alliances as a pragmatic strategy in tackling issues of immigration and domestic violence. The chapter documents the role of Abasindi in the 1981 Moss Side uprisings against racism and the contribution of the Manchester Black Access Course, developed in the wake of the riots, to the politicization of Black women.

Chapter 8 concludes the book by acknowledging and celebrating 'ordinary women' who came together within Abasindi to achieve 'extraordinary' things. The authors draw on their personal reflections to demonstrate ways in which the academy and professional spaces have become sites of political activism for Black women, who are increasingly engaged in seizing opportunities to contribute to scholarship and the production of knowledge.

Chapter 2
The legacy of Black women's activism

Introduction

Identity and finding a voice are regarded as central to women's development. In their publication, *The Heart of the Race*, Bryan *et al.* (1985: 2) state that 'Our aim has been to tell it as we know it, placing our story within its history at the heart of the race, and using our own voices and lives to document the day-to-day struggles of Afro-Caribbean women in Britain over the past 40 years'. Lewis (1996: 170) insists that 'all women must tell their stories in their own words', and identifies oral life history as an avenue through which to accomplish this. The writings of African-American women further assert the right to speak out and reverse the devaluing and silencing of hundreds of years of racial and gendered subordination (Wisker, 2000: 59). Alice Walker's writing is concerned with rescuing Black women from silence through the establishment of sisterhood and the writing of what she terms 'womanist prose'. She sees the experiences of Black women in America as a series of movements from racial and sexual oppression to a state of consciousness, thus allowing them to have some control over their lives.

This evolutional process is both historical and psychological and consists of three interrelated cycles: suspension, assimilation and emergence. For African-Caribbean women in the UK, Alexander and Dewjee (1984) cite the use of letters, diaries, autobiographies, testimonies, photographs and drawings as important sources in the reclaiming of Black women's history, as in their research on the life of Mary Seacole. Based on the experiences of women from the 1960s onwards and reflecting a continuation of Black women's activism, as in the work of Una Marson, Amy Ashwood Garvey and Amy Jacques Garvey, this chapter sets out the social and political context that gave rise to the Abasindi Black Women's Cooperative.

Francia Messado

My sister used to say, 'It's as if you have two families – your biological family and Abasindi'. In so many ways she was right! Within this global family of beautiful, Black, strong, astounding women they are fundamentally akin to sisters, aunties, mothers, grandmothers and friends, with the blessings of our children. Being a member of Abasindi has been both a privilege and an opportunity. I was invited to Abasindi in 1979, then being a young mother without a sense of life direction. In observing and listening to the first conversations around the big brown wooden table, the first buzz word that still rings true for me today was *self-sufficiency*. Motivated by what I'd seen and heard – YES, self-sufficiency was definitely in action at Abasindi, hence my involvement, which in turn encouraged my learning, development and growth.

A sister-member once said 'I need Abasindi more than it needs me'. Upon reflection, I can definitely concur with that sentiment, as Abasindi was indeed a lifeline. We communicated, expressed, laughed, cried, shared problems and dreams, negotiated, made decisions and organized – always empowering one another in striving to make a holistic human difference.

There was so much to do and be a part of in Abasindi: Saturday school, summer school, crèche, hair plaiting, sewing, cultural groups including Kutamba and Abasindi Pan-African Drummers and Dancers, women's and cultural exchanges, immigration and political campaigns, the Cultural Shop, the Moss Side Arts Group and the Nia Centre, and fundraising events. Abasindi was also the village community centre in the heart of Moss Side and surrounding areas, opening its doors to everyone. Abasindi's Centre was used for church services and other celebratory life events including parties.

Over the years, the range of skills I learned assisted in my participation in a variety of roles. This included summer-school assistant, performer/workshop facilitator in dance/music, activist, chairperson, and project coordinator. It also led to many opportunities. For example, the Abasindi Drummers and Dancers have ranged from playing in solidarity with immigration campaigns in the local street of Princess Road, to performing at PANAFEST in Ghana.

> Abasindi has been fundamental in both my personal and my professional life. All was due to the selfless, priceless exchange of shared energies, the external progression of these amazing women's abilities and the results of collective achievement. Humble gratitude and *love* to all Abasindi women: warriors and empresses, role models, mentors, elders and youth, near and far, on earth and in spirit. I am truly blessed to be part of such an invaluable experience. It has enlightened me and instilled confidence and positive resilience. These treasured memories have helped me to evolve and they continue to inspire the woman I am today.

Striving and thriving

In his paper 'Better Mus' Come', Farrar (1989: 4) argues that community 'is the term used by people of all ethnic groups not simply to characterize the present or to demarcate "us" from "them", but to evaluate the present and the past and to carry dreams, hopes, yearnings for the future'. Symbolically it stands for the yearning for a better life, as in the civil rights struggles in America where Dr Martin Luther King declared that the 'Aftermath of nonviolence is the creation of the beloved community':

> Building the 'beloved community' is both the process and the hoped for outcome of individual and political empowerment. It is where we are going and how we will get there. It is the essence of Dr Martin Luther King Jr's dream: a caring community where race and class is transcended and social and economic justice is the rule and not the exception.
>
> (Lee, 2001: 1)

The building of 'beloved communities' by Black migrants in cities such as Manchester at the end of the Second World War was in part due to the rise in migration from the Caribbean islands to the North-West. This is not to deny that ever since the sixteenth century Black people have been inextricably linked to the structure of British society as both slaves and free men and women. Bryan *et al.* (1985) argue that:

> Our presence in eighteenth century England was an accepted reality. Black women and men were sold openly at auctions; the busts of 'blackamoors' emblems of the trade, commonly adorned local town halls. Black servants were common too, and our children were the inevitable appendages of slave Captains and

> high-society women. Freed and runaway slaves were conspicuous among London's beggars and were known as 'St Giles Blackbirds'. Though in constant fear of recapture, we lived side by side with the white working class, intermarrying with them and taking part in the life of the community.
>
> (Bryan *et al.*, 1985: 7–8)

However, the development of post-war migrant communities was signalled by the arrival of the *Empire Windrush* at Tilbury on 22 June 1948. Fryer (1984: 372–3) described the passengers on the *Empire Windrush* as 'Five Hundred pairs of Willing Hands', who then found themselves among those that would eventually be regarded as 'competitive intruders'. Glass and Pollins wrote:

> Coloured people are feared as competitive intruders; they are thought of as promoters of crime and carriers of disease; they are resented when they are poor; they are envied when they are resourceful and thrifty. They are looked down upon; they are patronised; occasionally they are treated just like everyone else.
>
> (Glass and Pollins, 1960: 120)

This fear of 'coloured' people was also translated into personal relations. In 1957 Collins reported that the arrival of West Indian women 'immigrants' was particularly welcomed by the British male 'who feels that she will provide a companion for the coloured male immigrant, who will keep away from British women' (cited in Webster, 1998: 61). Up until the 1950s, international migration was heavily dominated by men and this is seen as critical in explaining high levels of female-headed households in many of the Caribbean islands. These women could be found living independently within a close-knit community, or as head of an extended family that included their own children as well as those of other relatives or strangers. Similarly, in her discussion on women-headed units in West Africa, Ekejuiba (1995) applies the term 'hearthold-household' to describe a family unit that may exist independently or within an established household. This unit is demographically made up of women, children and dependants with shared responsibility for the caring and nurturing of other members of the hearthold.

MELANIE DUNCAN
When I think of Abasindi, I conjure up a picture: the red building symbolizing the blood that unites a people. My memories, random but empowering, come flooding back in all their splendour, answering questions that have only just come to mind. 'Ain't I a woman', an image, imprint in my thoughts, a picture of a stern woman, who demanded that in a time when she was not even observed as a human being, she be recognized as a woman. The women themselves were a force to be reckoned with. They were creative and strong, as was evident in their efforts to raise a family in the context of the group dynamics. There was always so much to do. As I reflect on my life as it is, I am not sure where I would find the time to do as much as the Abasindi ladies did and with such aplomb. From a child's eye view, women ran things, held down jobs, raised children, and did Abasindi.

'West Indians' and West Africans

The organizers of the 1945 Pan-African Conference held at the Chorlton Town Hall stated that one of the reasons for choosing Manchester was the fact that:

> Manchester had become quite a point of contact with the coloured proletariat in Britain, and we had made a name for ourselves in fighting various areas of discrimination ... Manchester was an expression of a mass movement intimately identified with the under-privileged sections of the coloured colonial populations.
> (Fryer, 1984: 347–9)

Britain's Black colonial population included the passengers on the *Empire Windrush*. These men, most of whom were Jamaican, had served in the British armed forces during the Second World War and viewed their journey as a return to the 'Motherland'. The brothers Mike and Trevor Phillips (1998) describe the event as:

> a journey through the gateway of history, on the other side of which was the end of Empire and a wholesale reassessment of what it meant to be British. To the majority of those aboard, their arrival in England represented a leap into the unknown, an adventure in which no one knew what they would find.
> (Phillips and Phillips, 1998: 4–6)

Euston Christian, Manchester's first Black Justice of the Peace, was among the passengers on the *Empire Windrush* who had come to England during the Second World War as a member of the Royal Air Force. After six months back in Jamaica, he returned to England on the *Empire Windrush*. He agreed to take up 'extended duties' with the RAF and served in it for several years. He was among those, including the late Ashton Douglas ('Mr Dougy'), Aubery Lawford and Pip Gore, who founded the West Indian Sports and Social Club in Moss Side. These men's love of cricket gave birth to a centre which has become one of the mainstays of Manchester's African-Caribbean community. The current work of Tom Nelson, Leon Smith and Cleveland Brady is a testament to this legacy. Even before the *Windrush* docked, many West African seamen had settled in areas such as Cheetham Hill and Salford. From the 1940s on, the number of servicemen and merchant seamen from the Caribbean islands and West Africa increased. Some began to move their families into Hulme, an area that provided much of the material for Friedrich Engels's study on the conditions of the working class in England.

The opportunity to survive and thrive was provided by a range of supportive networks that included GP Peter Milliard and Mr Harding, proprietor of a hostel in Hulme. These men provided cheap medical support and accommodation for Black seamen. Small businesses, shopkeepers, barbers and nightclub owners were among those who provided financial support to the community. Phillips (1975: 273) argues that 'it seems unlikely that the Black communities in any other British city would have been able to deploy the political, financial and organizational resources to host the 1945 Pan-African Congress'. The organizers of the conference cited another reason for choosing Manchester, namely Black people's contribution to the development of the city:

> You could say that we coloured people had a right there because of the age-old connections between cotton, slavery and the building up of cities in England. Manchester gave us ... an important opportunity to express and expose the contradictions, the fallacies and the pretentions that were at the very centre of empire.
>
> (Fryer, 1984: 347–8)

The delegates at this conference included Amy Ashwood Garvey who, along with her husband Marcus Garvey, co-founded the Universal Negro Improvement Association (UNIA). The conference began on 15 October, with a discussion of Britain's racial problems. Speaking as the chair of the session, Amy Ashwood observed that:

> A nation without great women is a nation frolicking in peril. Let us go forward and lift the degradations which rest on the Negro woman – God's most glorious gift to civilisation.
>
> (Swaby, 2010)

On the issue of race and gender, Amy Jacques, Marcus Garvey's second wife, acknowledged that Black women's experience of oppression was often distinguishable from that of Black men. She is thus seen as belonging to a legacy of Black female activists who were cognizant of the distinctive plight faced by Black women as a result of racial, gender and class oppression. Collins (1990: 151) describes her work as representing 'A form of Afrocentric feminist political activism essential to the struggle for group survival' that placed 'family, children, education and community at the center of ... political activism'.

The 'African Queen'

The subsequent development of the Black community in Moss Side during the 1960s was linked to its proximity to Trafford Park. Phillips (1975) observes that the...:

> Black population development after 1950 centred in Moss Side, partly because there were already some blacks established there, but more importantly, because it was reasonably handy for Trafford Park, one of the largest industrial complexes in Europe where cheap labour was always needed.
>
> (Phillips, 1975: 296)

The Number 53 bus, whose route took it from Moss Side to Trafford Park was christened the 'African Queen', by virtue of the fact that thousands of Manchester's Black workers travelled daily on it to badly paid, dirty and dangerous jobs. Black people in Manchester, as elsewhere in the country, were concentrated at the lower end of the labour market. According to one of the White church ministers who was invited to Manchester in 1953 by the bishop to work specifically with new arrivals from the West Indies:

> It was difficult getting jobs for the immigrants; employers didn't want to know at all about West Indians, shops were more difficult, the excuses then were that their customers were prejudiced. I remember a job that had to do with somebody to work with bananas, it was a wholesale Fruit Market and they didn't want a West Indian because their customers would probably object. I said well, don't you know that before you got the bananas,

they had been handled by West Indians and you didn't know the colour would run off on them?

(Roots Oral History Project, 1992: 40)

Black people's choice of where they lived was very restricted and many lived in multi-occupational houses with two or three families sharing a single kitchen. House prices rose steadily during the 1960s and finance companies' terms and conditions effectively exploited the ethnic minority residents' need for mortgages:

> In general ... banks and building societies had high refusal rates for black applicants in black neighbourhoods and in the area when mortgages were rationed, were using less stringent status criteria for white applicants. Lenders' stereotyping of preferences sustains the expectation that Asians and West Indians will only want to buy in areas where their community is concentrated, and that no whites will want to buy there or remain living there, which mirrors similar processes in the allocation of council housing.
> (Karn, 1983: 174–9)

Despite these difficulties, by 1969 the majority of Black people living in Moss Side/Hulme owned their own houses:

> I bought my first house and sold it after a year to buy a second. I remember the neighbours collecting a petition against me living in that area. I told them that my money paid for the house. The area was predominantly white but as time went by, the white owners sold to Black families and moved out of the area.
> (Roots Oral History Project, 1992: 16)

Based on interviews undertaken between 1989 and 1992, Sterling (1995) found that one of the social-cultural practices that early immigrants from the Caribbean islands brought with them to Britain was that of the 'partner'. He argued that because of the difficulties they faced in getting loans from banks and building societies, they had no choice but to resort to this traditional method of securing funds: 'By participating in partners they were able to "beat the system," by finding alternative ways of acquiring credit for purposes, initially of family reunions and access to housing' (Sterling, 1995: 654). This was certainly the case in Manchester:

> ... I had difficulty in securing accommodation and I started to understand what discrimination meant. I would see 'Vacancy' marked on the windows, but when I knocked on the door to

make enquiries, white landlords use to slam the door in my face ... I was eventually offered a room by this old white fellow who kept foreign students ... My landlord was friendly but I was desperate to be amongst my own people. This I did when I moved to Moss Side. I was able to join what is call 'Pardner or Susu'. I was able to save and could send for my wife soon after I arrived here. As soon as she arrived I bought a house with a £75 deposit and thereafter an instalment of £11 monthly.
(Roots Oral History Project, 1992: 12)

In 1968, Manchester City Council announced plans for rehousing the entire area. In response, a political campaign opposing the destruction of the area was mounted by the Housing Action Group. All their subsequent attempts failed and from 1970–4 Black people were dispersed and Moss Side effectively demolished. By 1973, 80 per cent of West African and Caribbean sole traders on Denmark Road, Princess Road, Monton and Darcy Street had also gone out of business. Faced with rapidly rising house prices in other areas and continued racial discrimination, most Black householders accepted tenancy from the local authority, because compensation payments were generally too low to purchase an equivalent size house elsewhere:

Our first home was in Meadow Street in Moss Side ... soon after I bought my house and had tenants in my spare rooms, I lost this house under compulsory purchase order from the court. They paid less than what the house was worth and I subsequently made a loss on it.
(Roots Oral History Project, 1992: 8)

The proportion of Black owner-occupiers fell dramatically. The total number of Black people to become council tenants rose from 291 in 1970 to 789 in 1971, and by 1975 most Black people in Moss Side and Hulme were council tenants. However, this dispersal was short-lived as large numbers of Black people refused to be relocated on housing estates away from the city centre. Night workers living outside the area often found that little or no public transportation was available at nights. Furthermore, the local schools were also reluctant to accept Black children from the inner city (Phillips, 1975).

Since the early 1990s redevelopment has yet again involved the disruption, and at times destruction, of established community networks. The groups that were based in the old St Mary's School, re-named Moss Side People's Centre, included the Moss Side Adventure Playground, the Family Advice Centre and Abasindi Cooperative. The building has since been converted into a privately owned nursery. Despite these changes, the spirit of 'beloved community' remains a vibrant aspect of life in Moss Side, as was evident in the 2012 celebrations of the life of Kath Locke, one of the founder members of Abasindi.

Black women's activism

The early experiences of Black women workers have been described as a 'long catalogue of hardship', and that provided fertile soil for the growth of Black women's activism. In Manchester, many of the women travelling on the Number 53 bus were to be found working in food production and packaging. Others worked in the clothing industry, parts of which were notorious for sweatshop conditions and low wages. One woman told us in an interview:

> I was doing a job, it was a menial job but there were white people and although we were all doing exactly the same kind of work, they use to get more money than us the coloured ones ... most days we do exactly the same amount, they still got more money than I did.
>
> (Watt, 2002: 169)

Lewis (1993) argues that in the absence of capital investment, the substitution of cheap labour from the Caribbean and the Indian subcontinent, as well as indigenous women workers, represented an attempt by Britain to deal with the effects of its long-term decline. Alongside this intensification of the rate of exploitation of women workers there was the added dimension of the sexual division of labour. This took place irrespective of women's racial origin and had the effect of determining the occupation into which they would be absorbed. For Black women:

> the ideology of racism and the practice of racialism were to intertwine with the ideology and practice of sexism, both of which were to impact on the structural characteristics of the British economy to determine the industrial and occupational location of Black women workers.
>
> (Lewis, 1993: 74)

One woman went so far as to describe her experience in 1964 as a form of twentieth-century 'slavery'. This was at a factory in Manchester making crisps, from which she was eventually sacked for taking a stance against working in an environment that denied workers, the majority of whom were Black women, the right to go to the 'Ladies' without the permission of the White female supervisor. This was at a time when, according to Bhabha and Shutter (1994: 38–9):

> The only kind of work that most black women were able to find was in industries where low pay and bad conditions prevailed. These included the textile industry – both the large mills in the North West of England and the small, family-based sweated businesses in the East of London – and hospitals and other service industries where, more often than not, they worked as cleaners or orderlies.
>
> (Bhabha and Shutter, 1994: 38–9)

The racialized practice of employers and some unions fed the misapprehension that Black women workers were working for 'pin money' (Lewis, 1993: 82). It was standard practice for migrant women to be recruited at the bottom end of the occupational ladder. Thus Black women were excluded from working in shops or offices (Webster, 1998: 130). This was the experience of Una Marson who migrated to England during the 1930s. Despite her educational achievements and professional credentials, in the search for office work she found herself confronted with the harsh realities of racial discrimination:

> I tried to register for work as a stenographer. One agent told me that she didn't register black women because they would have to work in offices with white women. Another agent tried to find me a position and he told me though my references were excellent, firms did not want to employ a black stenographer.
>
> (Jarrett-Macauley, 1998: 51)

Within the National Health Service, Black women were employed mainly as domestic cleaners and canteen workers. Those who wished to train as nurses were often rejected or channelled away from the State Registered training towards the lower-status State Enrolled qualification. There was also a tendency for Black nurses from the Caribbean to be concentrated in specific areas such as geriatrics, learning disability and mental health. Similarly, African doctors were over-represented in areas of psychiatry and geriatrics. Furthermore, there was a noticeable absence of Black people in areas of physiotherapy, chiropody, speech therapy and radiotherapy. For those who came directly from the Caribbean to train as State Registered Nurses (SRN), one woman described it as a period fraught with 'difficulties':

> I arrived in England in 1951, to pursue a course in nursing at a hospital in London. During my career as a student nurse, I came across a series of problems with nursing sisters who make you go to the sluice all day to wash wastes from incontinent patients. It was very difficult then to figure out why it was always the few black nurses and Irish who got sent down to the sluice ... There were other aspects of nursing duties to be done, but invariably you end up in the wretched sluice, either cleaning bed pans or washing the messy bed sheets. Freezing cold, freezing but you had to accept it, though you knew it was wrong. You would be upset but you couldn't show it. It was difficult, very difficult.
>
> (Roots Oral History Project, 1992: 21)

A study during the 1980s found that 61 per cent of the qualified nursing workforce was from overseas. Within this group, Irish and Malaysians were often State Registered Nurses (SRN), ward sisters and nursing officers, while Caribbean and Filipino women were likely to be State Enrolled Nurses (SEN) or nursing auxiliaries:

> I began my nursing career as a cadet nurse. At first I did not enjoy nursing because I was pushed into doing the SEN course. During the period of my training I realized that not only was I getting top marks but some of the other trainees were quite dumb and I was having to help them out. After completing my training, I decided that nursing wasn't for me ... Although I successfully completed my first degree in Social Administration, at the time a career change was not possible so I returned to nursing on a part-time basis. At this stage I made the decision to upgrade my nursing qualification to that of Registered General Nurse ... Having completed the RGN in 1993 within the space of six years I was on the 'G' grade. However, I was aware of the fact that many Black nurses who had successfully completed their conversion course were still on the lower 'D' grade. A few years later, I obtained a further degree in specialist nursing, and my work to date has included that of a specialist nurse counsellor.
>
> (Watt, 2002)

The children of these early migrants from the Caribbean islands had similar experiences, as in the case of the British-born woman whose parents came to England in 1954. This woman's mother was among those who had the opportunity to train as an SRN. Having worked on a voluntary basis with the elderly, she decided to train as a nurse. During the course of the interview she was asked whether or not she knew the difference between a State Registered and State Enrolled Nurse. In response she told the interviewers that her mother and other women in her family were State Registered Nurses. The members of the interviewing panel responded by informing her that SENs were good bedside nurses and as such they regarded her as a suitable candidate for this category of nursing. Although extremely upset, she did not realize that this rejection was based primarily on the colour of her skin and thought that the interviewers just did not like her. She knew that some of the children had not liked her at school because whenever someone called her 'nigger', she would, as she said, 'batter' them, and the headmistress would respond by telling her that she had a 'chip on her shoulder'. This was not the same with the interviewing panel because they had only just met her and she was really at a loss as to why they were so unpleasant towards her. She nevertheless remained undeterred and subsequently trained as an SRN at one of the London hospitals. As a State Registered Nurse, midwife and health visitor with an MA in Women's Studies, she has worked in various management positions within the field of health care.

The late Louise Da-Cocodia was one of the early post-war migrants who came to England to train as a State Registered Nurse (SRN):

> After obtaining my State Registration, I undertook midwifery training and subsequently completed the health visitor's course, then I took up a senior post in Berkshire. I came to Manchester to take up a post as Assistant Superintendent of District Nurses. In my senior post, it became apparent that some of the white nurses under my supervision didn't like receiving orders from me ... There were resentments, because you'd see them sort of thinking, 'And who do you think you are you so and so.' Although there was nothing they could do about it because I had the authority.
> (Roots Oral History Project, 1992: 21)

In addition to her work with the National Health Service, not to mention the care of her two children, Richard and Sarah Nisemi Da-Cocodia, Louise Da-Cocodia became the chairperson for the West Indian Overseas Coordinating Committee (WIOCC) in 1984. Two years later she co-founded Cariocca Enterprise Ltd, Arawak-Walton housing. In 1989 she was awarded an honorary master's degree by the Victoria University of Manchester for services to nursing and the community. In 1990 she was nominated to the Manchester Magistrates Bench where she served for 14 years. Based on her activities in the field of racial justice she received the Manchester Race

Louise Da-Cocodia

Award (1995) for improving race relations in the city. The same year she became a member of the General Synod of the Church of England. Four years later she was appointed Deputy Lord Lieutenant for Greater Manchester. Having received a British Empire Medal in 1992, Louise Da-Cocodia was awarded an MBE in 2005 for her tireless service to the local community. Following a short period of illness she unexpectedly passed away on 13 March 2008. As she had been one of the founder members of Cariocca Education Trust, and in acknowledgement of her work, the organization was re-named the Louise Da-Cocodia Education Trust.

The experiences of all these women in the NHS were not unlike the position of Mary Seacole, the once forgotten and now celebrated Jamaican nurse who travelled at her own expense to the Crimea in 1855 with the sole purpose of volunteering her services as a nurse. Her offer was rejected, and despite Seacole's extensive nursing skills she was not among the 38 nurses selected by Florence Nightingale to accompany her to the Crimean War (Day, 1994) and had to fund her journey to, and work in the Crimea.

In his foreward to Mary Seacole's 1857 autobiography, William Howard Russell, an influential journalist and special correspondent for the *Times* wrote, 'I have witnessed her devotion and her courage ... and I trust that England will never forget the one who has nursed her sick, who sought out her wounded to aid and succour them, and who performed the last offices for some of her illustrious dead' (www.maryseacoleappeal.org.uk/about.htm). Mary Seacole was nevertheless forgotten. So much so that in 1977 an approach by the Manchester Black Women's Mutual Aid to host the first Roots Festival on 'The Life and Times of Mary Seacole' at a local secondary school was rejected on the grounds that no such person had existed. According to one of the members of the Manchester Black Women's Mutual Aid, the teachers threatened to walk out, claiming that the women in the group were just troublemakers. Following the success of this first Roots Festival, held at the West Indian Centre, Carmoor Road, it was decided that it should be an annual event. After the arrival of a new and supportive headteacher, for the next 12 years the week-long Roots Festival was held at the school that had initially rejected it. The themes included 'The International Year of the Child', 'Harriet Tubman' and 'Growing Up in Multi-Racial Britain'.

Abasindi

Sudbury (1998: 98) argues that Black women's organizations are spaces in which Black women can create oppositional and empowering narratives of self. The Organisation for Women of Asian and African Descent (OWAAD) 1978–82 was thus seen as the catalyst for the creation of a number of Black women's organizations throughout the country. In Manchester this included the Manchester Black Women's Cooperative, the Manchester Black Women's Mutual Aid, the Moss Side and Hulme Women's Action Forum, and Sojourners. The Manchester Black Women's Cooperative was initially established to

Mama Edwards (Elouise Edwards)

create a place for women to develop office skills geared towards meeting the training and employment needs of young Black mothers. It also provided the space for young men and women to become politically involved with the development of their community, in particular relating the liberation struggles in various countries in Africa to their own experiences of racism and class discrimination. In 1979 members of the group undertook a lengthy and critical review of the organization and concluded that although it was located in the community the membership was not representative of the community. They acknowledged that while community can be a place for women's activism, it can also be a place that limits women's control and choice. The organization needed to provide space and opportunities for women's political growth and development. Elouise Edwards, one of the founder members of the Black Women's Mutual Aid, also stated that few of us are chosen as 'leaders' and women's contributions are generally ignored or played down – Abasindi aimed to redress this.

On 1 January 1980 Manchester Black Women's Cooperative reformed as Abasindi, meaning 'Survivors' in the language of the Zulu people of South Africa. The members of the Cooperative chose this name and its motto 'Zizelewe Ukusinda' as a tribute to the strength, resilience and competence of Black women, in particular those in Africa and the African Diaspora that were actively involved in struggles against the dehumanizing and oppressive forces of apartheid, neo-colonialism, racism and sexism. Abasindi was established at a time when the government was focusing on the need for 'community involvement' and 'self-help'. The government also pointed to the importance of involving ethnic minority groups in the process of regeneration. While recognizing that self-help and voluntary projects alone could not change the socio-economic conditions of Black people living in areas such as Moss Side and Hulme, Abasindi nevertheless acknowledged the need for women's involvement in community-based projects. During this period the organization also constituted what Collins (1990: 223) describes as potential sanctuaries where individual Black women were able to develop empowering narratives of self. It is this source of nurturing and activism that enabled a number of women to confidently return to education by enrolling on access-to-degree courses. They duly completed their university studies and moved on to paid employment in a range of professional areas.

> **MARIA NOBLE**
> Whenever I think about Abasindi I feel a warm glow. This emanates firstly I think from the sisterhood I still feel for those women who were involved with the group. The second element is to do with remembering the strength of political activism that was happening across so many different fields during Abasindi's lifetime. Everything from opposing the 'sus' laws and police harassment of Black people, through challenging mainstream feminism; for example at the time when women's right to choose abortion was high on the agenda for White women, Black women were fighting its imposition and the forced sterilizations and sexual assault on ethnic minority women by immigration officials.
>
> Belonging to Abasindi taught me that grassroots organizing and activism can have a real effect and I've continued to work with my local community. As Abasindi we were involved with a number of

anti-deportation campaigns in support of African-Caribbean and Asian women, all of which were successful. Our Saturday and summer schools are still remembered by those who attended, now adults with their own children, as instilling pride and confidence. Abasindi Drummers and Dancers not only contributed to the cultural awareness and fitness of the women and girls involved, but offered a vibrant spectacle to innumerable fundraising, women's movement and community events.

A younger friend of mine asked me to tell her about Abasindi, so I asked her what she knew already. She said that she knew that it involved a strong group of women, but also that it was seen as lesbian and anti-men. I laughed out loud! I marvelled at how homophobia and sexism had come together in that perception to negate the status of the group.

I think we recognized that ours was a radical grouping, but never took on the label 'feminist', although there were members who defined themselves as feminist. The group was certainly very diverse, involving older established community activists, students, local working women, girls; Rastafarian, religious and atheist; women who just wanted to do something useful with their time. This grouping taught me that labels don't define individuals, it's their relationships and interactions with others that give the fuller picture. Our defining terms were Black and women, yet our concerns and actions were about improving the quality of life for our whole community.

It is great to see an upsurge of activism to challenge the self-serving greed and callousness of the ruling interests in the world. Each individual is made up of a complex mix of identities, today referred to as intersectionality, but I have learned to be cautious about becoming too hooked on the language we use. Working with all sorts of people, I've realized that it is behaviours, actions and outcomes that matter more than words. Being involved with Abasindi I learnt that doing is what makes the difference. It is more important than all the thinking and talking that frames one's actions.

I was one of only a few lesbians associated with Abasindi and one of the strengths of the group was that we drew on aspects of our individual identity and interests to be involved with a broad base of activism with a wide range of people. This has left me with an openness to talking to people and a willingness to make common cause with different groupings in order to work for the common good. This was a key transformation for me as experiences of racism had left me closed and self-protective in my earlier life.

Members of Abasindi bridged many different campaigns – Greenham Common, the Miners' dispute, seeking medical provision to tackle sickle-cell anaemia, tackling racial and gender discrimination in education, arguing for appropriate provision for Black children in care. We did solidarity work with the Nicaraguan socialists, anti-apartheid activists, Women Worldwide. We hosted cultural events and built links with cultural groups in Africa and the Caribbean, supported community-led initiatives such as the mentoring of school children, the Roots Family History Project and the annual Roots Festival that ran for several years, and gained a blue plaque in recognition of the 1945 Pan-African Congress. We backed a hostel for Black women survivors of domestic abuse. We participated in the short-lived national organizations, the Organisation of Women of African and Asian Descent (OWAAD) and the National Black Lesbian Support Group, as well as Manchester-based Black Sisters and local women's celebrations.

All these involvements contributed to our political awareness and built up skills and confidence among the women involved with Abasindi, but the bedrock for me was the weekly Friday meeting, which provided succour against some of the hard times that were confronting us all. If laughter is the best medicine, we certainly had a lot of it at these meetings, along with no small amounts of alcohol and cigarettes – not such healthy options. We talked about anything and everything, testing ideas and opinions. A number of great learning points for me were instilled by the late Kath Locke: we have our history and need to keep it in mind, learn from it and build on it. I can go on learning throughout my life from people and courses and through thinking. As a group we need to control funding, rather than let it control us.

I continue to act on these lessons. I was involved in the development of the Ahmed Iqbal Ullah Race Relations Archive/Resource Centre and Education Trust. I research and present talks on Black History. I'm active in building up social capital in my community, which is based on the efforts of local people, backed by appropriate funding pools.

The legacy of Black women's activism

In cautioning against taking ongoing funding Kath used to say, 'The state doesn't pay you to oppose it'. Indeed the state now pays community groups to keep its members in line and to denounce those 'radicals' who challenge state actions. Our lives are now under closer state scrutiny than ever before, for both legitimate and illegitimate reasons. The gains in equality that we made in the twentieth century – education, pay and conditions, housing quality, justice, anti-discrimination laws – are all under dire threat. Thanks to my grounding with my sisters in Abasindi I was under no illusions. We have to fight for rights and keep fighting to protect our gains.

Abasindi worked collaboratively with organizations such as the Manchester Black Women's Mutual Aid and the Moss Side and Hulme Women's Action Forum on a range of community development initiatives. The organization's work with the Moss Side and Hulme Women's Action Forum included the 1997 'Women as Role Model' Conference. As part of the European Year of Anti-Racism and International Women's Week, this conference was organized in celebration of the lives and achievements of Black women in Manchester.

Alima, Pauline, Rose, Yvonne, Abena, Maria, Coco, Diana and Kath get together at Alima's place, Crondall Street, Moss Side

The event was chaired by the late Louise Da-Cocodia, a founder member of the Moss Side and Hulme Women's Action Forum (MOSHWAF). In her opening address she concluded: 'The greatest challenge of the conference was to give voice to local women and women everywhere whose experience and aspirations go untested'. The speakers at the conference included Sharon Beck, who spoke about the lack of recognition in management courses on issues of sexism and racism and its impact on the lives of women aspiring to management positions. On the issue of Black women's position in areas of management, the 1997 campaign of the Commission for Racial Equality found that traditionally Black women were more reluctant than men to complain about institutional racism.

At the 'Women as Role Model' Conference, Val Blake highlighted the need for Black women to identify and celebrate their achievements. Carol Baxter emphasized the importance of recognizing and celebrating the contributions of Black women in the building of the country's National Health Service. Having mentored and supported two young women from an early age, Wilma Deane pointed out that even when as women we appear to have achieved success, our need for positive role models continues throughout life. The conference was also an opportunity to pay tribute to women activists such as Elouise Edwards and the late Kath Locke. Judy Craven talked about the ways in which these women had inspired and guided her. Bryan *et al.* further argue that:

> If we are to gain anything from our history and from our lives in this country which can be of practical use to us today, we must take stock of our experiences, assess our responses – and learn from them. This will be done by listening to the voices of the mothers, sisters, grandmothers and aunts who established our presence here. And by listening to our own voices.
> (Bryan *et al.*, 1985: 2)

Judy spoke about her experiences as an adult-education tutor working with women who, because they had no educational qualifications, would often describe themselves as 'only a housewife'. In conversation it was not unusual for the women to start with a list of things they could not do, yet it was obvious to her that they were involved in a range of complex activities both at home and within the wider community. She concluded that:

> It is proven in communities all over the globe that one of the things we women excel in is fostering, encouraging and drawing the potential out of sisters and the people around us. This is

something we should be celebrating and if we get the GCSE in English or the degree, that is good and wonderful; but if we feel that we have supported and developed somebody else this is the real achievement.

('Women as role models', 1997: 15)

In commenting on the findings of her own small-scale research on Black women's definition of achievement, one of the speakers found that the women in her study had different views on the concept of achievement. These included staying sane, being a good mother and creating a stable base for the family. The speaker argued that to encourage Black women to redefine achievement is not to diminish the concept generally or academic achievement in particular, but rather to recognize that for many women, there are far greater achievements in their lives outside of academia. It was therefore important for them to recognize and value all aspects of their life experiences and to acknowledge that one of the characteristics of Black women in history was their ability to assess their situation and plan strategies aimed at overcoming adversity, thus allowing them to move away from negative situations to a position of hope, faith and strength. Cobham (1990) argues that these are women whose experiences have been portrayed by Campbell in African-Caribbean poetry as 'history makers', as 'women stonebreakers', as 'hammers and rocks'. As 'builders' they are both the 'hammers which provide the power and the rocks which receive the blow'.

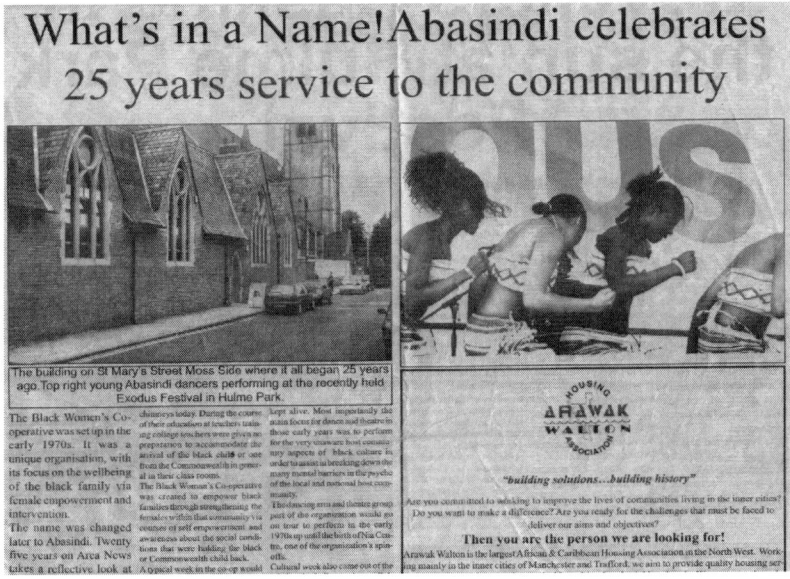

Chapter 3
Cultural expressions of resilience

From where
We do not know
We find the strength to crawl off the back shelf
Dragging the age-old mantles behind us:
Low achiever
Will not go far
Chip on shoulder
We have landed in the mire of history
And when we laugh if off
Our humour is considered intrusively loud
Fearfully aggressive
So we stop smiling
At those we do not know
Do not want to know
And the distance
Deepens over the years
But in the secret place of our dreams
Hope is never a stranger
We plot
Not like mutineers
We plan like generals
Determined to stop this war
We study
Write
Snip
At frugal budgets
Yet still we fashion ourselves
Sophisticate our styles
So that we may never be seen as
Third class
Because this ladder has missing rungs
We stumble

> But still we ascend
> The heavens may be out of reach
> But achievement
> Like retribution
> Is the goal of possibility.
> We are warriors
> Amazonians
> Mothers
> Wives
> Sisters
> Friends
> Standing at the edge of tides
> We would never exchange for anything
> Black and as beautiful as we are.
> ('Black and Beautiful as We Are', SuAndi © 2014)

Introduction

Resilience can be described as the 'ability to climb more times than you slip or fall by discovering faith, comfort and inner power'. The celebrated African-American civil rights activist, poet and writer Maya Angelou stated that 'To be successful is to be constant, to be patient and resilient – to accept things as they are. Resilience means ... laying claim to your spirit' (Riley, 2002: 243). This chapter explores the ways in which the women of Abasindi, by way of their many cultural expressions, have been resilient in withstanding and challenging racism and gendered forms of discrimination. Abasindi women laid claim to their spirit but they did not accept things as they were.

Beckles (1989) coined the terms 'natural rebel' and 'rebel woman' to describe the experiences of enslaved and oppressed Black women whose power has been associated with their ability to transmit cultural norms and practices. This form of power has no economic or political links. Neither is it based on the domination of women. It is a struggle of resistance and that which has been central in ensuring the survival of the group (Hill Collins, 1998). Nanny of the Maroons is noted for her legacy of resistance and resilience. She was an exceptional woman whose power was underpinned by material and cultural factors. Culturally she drew on the tradition of the Ashanti Queen-Mother, and materially on the control that African women had over agriculture (Sistren Theatre Collective and Ford-Smith: xv, xiv, xvi). In continuing along the path of resistance and resilience, Abasindi

Cooperative provided an opportunity for Black women to be proactively involved in both the development of self and of their wider community.

Historical expressions of resilience

Alice Walker (cited in Washington, 1982) argued that experiences of suspension, assimilation and emergence are the three cyclical stages that are associated with Black women's movement away from being victims of society and men to gaining control over their lives. Based on her personal interpretation of Black women's history in America, the stage of suspension refers to women during the nineteenth and early twentieth centuries. In her discussion of women who are in a state of suspension, Alice Walker argues that they are, in the words of Zora Neale Hurston, 'the mules of the world' (Russell, 1982). Sojourner Truth's speech at the 1851 Women's Convention in Akron, Ohio echoes the determination and resilience of these women, despite the fact that they were victims of racial and sexual oppression:

> That man over there says that a woman need to be helped into carriages, and lifted over ditches, and to have the best place everywhere. Nobody ever helped me into carriages, or over mud puddles, or give me a best place ... And ain't I a woman? Look at me. Look at my arm! I have ploughed and planted and gathered into barns, and no man could head me ... And ain't I a woman? I could work as much and eat as much as a man when I could get it, and bear the lash as well ... And ain't I a woman? I have borned thirteen children and seen them most all sold into slavery. And when I cried out with a mother's grief, none but Jesus heard ... And ain't I a woman?
>
> (Sojourner Truth, quoted in Davis, 1981: 61)

Amy Jacques Garvey of Jamaica, too believed that Black women's experiences of what King (1988) termed 'multiple jeopardy' compelled them to cultivate inner strengths that rendered them natural leaders in the fight for equality. As a leading Pan-Africanist and Black nationalist for over 50 years, she held the post of Secretary General for of the Universal Negro Improvement Association (UNIA). Based on the community, social and economic development model, UNIA – along with the African Communities League – was among the most powerful Black organizations of the early twentieth century. The African Communities League was the business arm of the organization and established the Negro Factories Corporation, which was responsible for managing UNIA's laundries, restaurants, tailoring and millinery establishments, printing press and doll factory. The doll factory was established to ensure that Black children had access to Black dolls. This was regarded as essential to the development of high levels of self-esteem, positive self-concept and pride in being Black (Carlton-LaNey, 2001: 81).

Although she was often described as Marcus Garvey's companion and 'nurturing spouse', Amy Garvey is surely one of the most remarkable women in history. In an effort to ensure racial survival Amy Garvey was among the women who developed a 'culture of resistance essential to the struggle for group survival (Collins, 1990: 147). This form of resistance offered Black people an alternative to prevailing racist, classist and sexist ideologies. From 1924 to 1927, Amy Jacques Garvey was the associate editor of the UNIA newspaper *The Negro World* and was responsible for introducing the page 'Our women and what they think'. The page included contributions not only from women in America, but also articles, poetry and letters from women in the Caribbean and different countries in Africa. In her article on 'Women as leaders', she describes Black women as the ones who have 'borne the rigors of slavery, the deprivations consequent on a pauperized race, and the indignities heaped upon a weak and defenceless people? Yet she has suffered all with fortitude and stands ever ready to help in the onward march to freedom and power.'

Matthews (1979) is critical of the tendency to minimize the work of Black women who played an integral role in the shaping of the Garvey movement. While maintaining that the Jamaican feminist movement of the 1930s and 1940s was nurtured within the Garvey movement, Ford-Smith (1988) found little difference from the ideal image upheld by dominant colonial ideology. During the period of Marcus Garvey's incarceration on charges of mail fraud in connection with the Black Star Line, Amy Garvey published volume two of *The Philosophy and Opinions of Marcus Garvey* and two volumes of his poetry, *The Tragedy of White Injustice* and *Selections from the Poetic Meditations of Marcus Garvey*. The proceeds from the sale of these publications were used towards Garvey's defence. After his death in 1940, Amy Jacques continued the struggle for Black Nationalism and played an instrumental role in the organization of the fifth Pan-African Congress, which was held at the Chorlton Town Hall in Manchester in 1945. She was one of the sponsors of the sixth Pan-African Congress in Tanzania in 1974. In 1963, she published her own book, *Garvey and Garveyism*, and later published two collections of essays, *Black Power in America* and *The Impact of Garvey in Africa and Jamaica*. In her article on the role of women in liberation struggles, Amy Jacques wrote:

> As a Black woman I was trained by my father, who lived in Cuba for years and spoke Spanish fluently; he also lived in Baltimore. He married my mother, and settled down in Jamaica, West Indies. For five years they had no children; so my mother prayed for a 'son and heir.' I came a girl, but my Dad trained me as if I were a boy. He took me around the property, explained to me how tobacco was grown and cured, taught me to use a gun to shoot stray goats. On Sundays, after dinner, he would collect his foreign newspapers, and I had to get a dictionary, and read editorials and news items; he would explain everything to me and answer all my questions. Sometimes he would give me an essay to write on a news item or article. This made me learn to think independently on world affairs and to analyse situations. So when I met Marcus Garvey the International Black mass Leader, he found in me an understanding and dedicated partner.
>
> (Jacques Garvey, 1972: 109–12)

Prior to her death in 1973, Amy Garvey was awarded the Institute of Jamaica Musgrave Gold Medal.

The 1940s and 1950s are described as the period of assimilation and are associated with Black women's experiences of psychic violence. This was a consequence of their desire for White acceptance at the expense of their own racial identity. Within the British context, it was a time when the Jamaican poet and journalist Una Marson was being described as:

> … a major figure in 20th century feminist black and literary histories. Her story arcs towards untouched visions for black people and for women and confronts the complexities of 'identity' in the modern world. And yet it has been erased because it is alternative, and discredited because it is critical. So often, even now, Black women of Una's stature appear only as token women in black texts or as token Blacks in feminist ones. When their contributions are noted, they might be represented superwomen – separate from their peers.
>
> (Jarrett-Macauley, 1998: viii)

Born in 1905, Una Marson encouraged women to develop their intellect and extend their activities beyond home and work. She was one of the founder members of the Jamaica Business Women Association (JBWA), and was among those who gave evidence to the West Indian Royal Commission on the condition of women in the British Caribbean. The Commission was

Cultural expressions of resilience

appointed in 1938 as a direct result of the labour rebellions in Jamaica and the other Caribbean islands (Shepherd, 1999). In 1932 Marson arrived in England aboard the SS *Jamaica Settler*. Within three years she had become a leading Black feminist activist in London. At the request of the Women's Social Service Club in 1935 she attended the 12th Annual Congress of the International Alliance of Women for Suffrage and Equal Citizenship. This event took place in Turkey and was attended by over 250 delegates. In commenting on her speech to the Congress, the *Manchester Guardian* reported that: 'This negro woman of African origin from the former slave world of Jamaica brought a new note into the assembly and astonished them by the vigour of her intellect and her feminist optimism' (Jarrett-Macauley, 1998: 87–91). As a Black nationalist and feminist writer she made several attempts to organize women into an active force in the nationalist movement through cultural expression. Sistren Theatre Collective attributes their existence to Marson's pioneering work in the use of her own experiences as the raw material for her poetry and drama. Marson also emphasized the 'link between art and nationalist struggle' (Sistren Theatre Collective and Ford-Smith, 1986: xxiv).

Walker's third cycle consists of 'emergent' women who were influenced by the political activism of the 1960s and 1970s. It was a period when African-Americans such as herself were encouraged by Black activists and musicians to 'Think Black, Talk Black, Create Black, Buy Black, Vote Black and Live Black' (Gilroy, 1987: 176–7). In Manchester the period of Walker's emergent women also gave rise to the activism of women such as the late Mama Innis, Ada Philips, Shirley Innis, Paula May, Olive Morris, Louise Da-Cocodia and Kath Locke.

Of all the women to have played a role in the success of the Abasindi Cooperative, it was Kath Locke and her political philosophy that was its driving force. The university

Olive Morris

law lecturer Paul Okojie is a long-standing friend of Abasindi who stood beside us in many of our human rights struggles. He knew Kath well. Below he reflects on her contribution to improving the lives of Black people in Manchester.

> ### KATH LOCKE 1928–91: THE POLITICS OF RESISTANCE
>
> Kath Locke was born in Manchester in 1928, but lived her early years in Blackpool. She remembered her school years in Blackpool and how her school deprived her – for racist reasons – of a place in a grammar school although she passed the 11+ examination. This had an unforgettable effect on her life and strongly influenced her politics and activism. In a video conversation with her just before her death, she recalled her parents' effort to right this cruel racism only for them to be thrown into a Kafkaesque world that led nowhere. Her parents were dealing with a school system lacking in accountability and transparency.
>
> In her early teens Kath returned with her parents to the red-brick two-up, two-down terraced houses of Moss Side, Manchester. Moss Side at the time had a large Irish immigrant population and some East European Jewish communities. African and Caribbean people started to settle in Moss Side from the 1930s and in large numbers after the war. She returned to a changed Moss Side – a concentric zone of Black Commonwealth citizens at the periphery of Manchester city centre; it mirrored experience elsewhere in Britain, where the more affluent White population moved to more prosperous suburbs. In spite of 'White flight', the Moss Side of her youth was a thriving community, culturally and commercially. For example, the Guyanese, Ras Makonnen, owned many business enterprises, earning enough income from them to be able to finance the fifth Pan-African Congress, held in Manchester in 1945. The area was buzzing with African-Caribbean clubs with names such as the Palm Beach, the Reno and the Nile, the Cotton Club and the Kroo Club.
>
> Although she travelled to many countries, including China, where she met some of the country's top political leaders, Manchester was Kath's home. She lived on the Alexander Park Estate, where she brought up her three children.

As a community activist, Kath was very concerned about the housing conditions on the estate. She campaigned vigorously against the council's neglect of housing, organizing petitions and leading demonstrations and marches. In the late 1960s and early 1970s Manchester Council eventually responded by improving the housing stock in the estate. This proved to her that the balance of power can be tilted in favour of political activism and solidarity. She was the perpetual idealist and an inspiration to many young people.

Kath believed strongly in the power of the community to change their situation. At the heart of this belief is the idea of self-empowerment – the Abasindi Black Women's Cooperative was an example. She would enumerate the conditions for achieving self-improvement: clarity of purpose, not keeping silent in the face of evil or injustice, social solidarity, sound organizational strategies and, above all, financial self-reliance. She was fastidious about the principle of not seeking financial help from any group to whom one is opposed. So Abasindi remained a self-financing entity. It was her cardinal belief that power relationships between the community and the economically powerful cannot be redressed if activists do not resist the temptation of the 'begging bowl'. She often recited the names of radical community groups that had become neutered in their politics as a result of financial dependency on the group they were supposed to be opposing. Pressure groups, she would argue, should remain true to their cause and avoid undermining their message by compromising.

The success of the campaign for the slum clearance on the Alexander Park Estate was a great lesson that shaped her activist politics. For example, following Kath's self-belief as an activist, the campaigners funded their own campaign. Also, when the women's group (which later metamorphosed into Abasindi Black Women's Cooperative) was first established, it was run by a male community 'leader' on patriarchal lines. Kath Locke and the other women had him removed and turned it into their vision of a community centre, the history of which is discussed in this book.

In spite of the undoubted success of the slum clearance on the Alexander Park Estate, Kath remained disappointed at the depth of social deprivation in Moss Side. She blamed this on several factors, key among these being the school system. She would cite, with approval, Bernard Coard's book, *How the West Indian Child is Made Educationally Subnormal in the British School System* (1971). The book had a dramatic impact on the ongoing debate about the causes of underachievement of Caribbean children in British schools and became part of the manifesto for those resisting racism in the education of Black children. Coard's view of Black children's experience in school chimed with Kath's experience as a school child in Blackpool. Although Coard's work was based on a study of inner London Schools, Kath believed the same was true of the experience of Black children in Manchester schools. She used to say that no child is uneducable and that teachers who think otherwise should not be in school. As with housing, she strongly supported parents whose children were facing expulsion or disciplinary hearings in school. Apart from racism in schools, Kath also believed that the lack of opportunity for Black people in the labour market due to racial discrimination was a major cause of poverty in the area.

It was through Kath that I first became aware of the work of Arthur Lewis in the Black community in Hulme and Moss Side. He was the Black Professor of Economics at Manchester University who won the Nobel Prize for Economics in 1979. She drew attention to his work to show how long the people of Moss Side had been forced to live with poverty and deprivation due to neglect by the civic authorities. She would remark time and again that it was not through lack of knowledge but wilful blindness. Professor Lewis came from Saint Lucia and like Kath he was concerned about the economic position of Black people in Manchester. He died in the same year as Kath, 1991. Both had wider concerns about the police, the criminal justice system and the prevailing racial discrimination. Following the 1981 Moss Side Uprising (during which Abasindi was the centre where those wounded by the Tactical Aid Group – a paramilitary force within the Greater Manchester Police – were taken for first aid treatment prior to going to hospital) Kath became an ardent campaigner against the abuse of police powers against Black people.

Kath Locke pondered all her life over what the community should do about racism. In a way, she provided the answer in the establishment of Abasindi. Visitors found that Abasindi was not only a community centre, but also a kind of school without borders and Kath was the Mwalimu, an inspiring community educator – she could be said to have embodied Paulo Freire's idea of communities as their own educators. Kath was a strong advocate of the Black community harnessing their social capital to respond to its myriad problems: schooling, housing, unemployment, racial discrimination and the menace of the National Front, and she regarded identity as the 'pull' that would bring the community together to act in their interest.

As well as her local activism, Kath was a political activist at the international level. This was most evident when she discussed the impact of the fifth Pan-African Congress, held in Manchester in 1945. Although she was too young to take part in the conference, she recalled with pride meeting some of the key conference delegates such as Jomo Kenyatta and Ras Makonnen through her father's connections. Throughout her life she believed that the problems facing Black people, whether local or international, could be solved through unity and collective solidarity.

She will always be remembered as one of Manchester's most powerful and feisty fighters for the people's rights.

Paul Okojie

Disconnections and reunification

Although most of the Abasindi members were born or had strong family links with the Caribbean, the sense of Africanness is what informed the individual and collective identity of the group, despite the disconnection and divisions that had been sown through colonialism. 'Colonisation is not satisfied merely with holding a people in its grip ... by a kind of perverted logic, it turns to the past of the oppressed people, and distorts, disfigures and destroys it' (Fanon, 1968: 70). In 1840-1, the decision by the Mayor of Kingston in Jamaica to ban John Canoe festivals during Christmas celebrations was based on what was seen as the festival's 'barbarous' African linkages. The mayor was of the view that the 'wild' dancing and the 'noisy' drumming had to be curtailed if the formerly enslaved were to acquire new habits of 'civilization' and decorum (Shepherd *et al.*, 1995: 286–7).

The disconnection from Africa was central to the experiences of Caribbean people. By placing Africa at the centre of its cultural expressions Abasindi provided women with the space to both 'recover' and 'discover'. This journey of reunification with the ancestors is in keeping with the fundamental tenets of traditional West African religious practices and ancient theological beliefs in the existence of two or more souls. The Yoruba people of Nigeria and the Fon of Dahomey identify four souls. The first is the life soul, which comes from the Supreme Being and enters us at the time of birth. The second is the personality soul, which differentiates us from each other. The third soul is the guardian soul, commonly referred to as the guardian angel. Fourth, there is the shadow soul, which is indistinguishable from the guardian soul. In the Caribbean, the belief in the hereafter is a mixture of both Christian and African practices. At death and after three days, the soul that comes from God goes back to God. The personality soul returns to the land of the ancestors and may be reborn repeatedly in children of the lineage. The guardian and/or shadow soul usually remains with the family for nine days, to ensure that all the funeral rites are completed. The soul may also stay indefinitely, depending on the circumstances in which death occurred. While taking their leave from the family they still remain in the land of the living and communicate with them either through dreams or visions (Barrett, 1976: 108).

The extent of the colonialist fear and opposition to traditional religious practices such as voodoo – derived from Vodun, the principal deity of the Yoruba people – can be seen in the following extract from a speech given by Jules Renkin, Governor of Kinshasa. This speech to the first group of missionaries to the Congo in 1883 was published in a Belgian newspaper in 1951:

> Reverend Father and dear Compatriots, the task, I ask you to accomplish is very delicate and demands much tact and diplomacy. Fathers you are going to preach the Gospel, but your preaching must be inspired by first, the interest of the Belgian State ... To do so, you will see that our savages be not interested in the riches that their soil possesses, in order that they will not want them ... You will cause them to follow the Saints who turned the other cheek. You will take them away from anything and act that procures them with the courage to confront us. I'm alluding myself here to their magic, i.e. Ju-Ju, Voodoo. They should feel like abandoning their Ju-Ju and you will do your best to take them.
>
> (Afrika Global Network, n.d.)

Obeah and Myal are two of the terms that were used in Jamaica to describe religious and quasi-religious activities among the enslaved. Section 3 of the 1760 Jamaica Obeah Act clearly pointed to the colonialist belief in a relationship between religion and rebellion (Alleyne, 1988: 83). Among

Cultural expressions of resilience

the explanations given for this association is the fact that whatever their ethnicity, the enslaved in preparing for war would invariably appeal to Loa Ogun, the Yoruba god of war (Campbell, 1990: 4).

'Naming' and 'renaming'

For the women of Abasindi, names were an important part of their identity. According to Woodward (1977: 1) 'identity gives us an idea of who we are and how we relate to others and to the world in which we live'. During the period of enslavement, 'un-naming' and 'renaming' of newly arrived enslaved people from Africa was one way in which slave owners established possession of people and their descendants, whom they regarded as their property. In George Dow's 1927 book, *Slave Ships and Slaving*, Edward Manning, who was a sailor on the slaver *Thomas Watson* is quoted as having said:

Atinuke (Tinu)

> I suppose they ... all had names in their own dialect, but the effort required to pronounce them was too much for us, so we picked out our favourites (slaves) and dubbed them *Main-stay, Cats head, Bulls eye, Rope-Yarn*, and various other sea phrases.
> (Fitzpatrick, 2012: 41)

Giving their children Yoruba, Zulu and Xhosa names such as Malaika, Olayinka, Dkizo, Nkosi, Thembikile, Zindiwe or Sibongile represented not only a 'recovery' of ancestral names but also an expression of Abasindi's support for struggles against apartheid in South Africa and colonialist oppression in other parts of Africa. Some of the women at Abasindi also adopted African names.

The process of re-naming was prevalent among African-Caribbean and African-American people during the Black Power era and the Civil Rights Movement in the 1960s and 1970s. Among African-Americans the

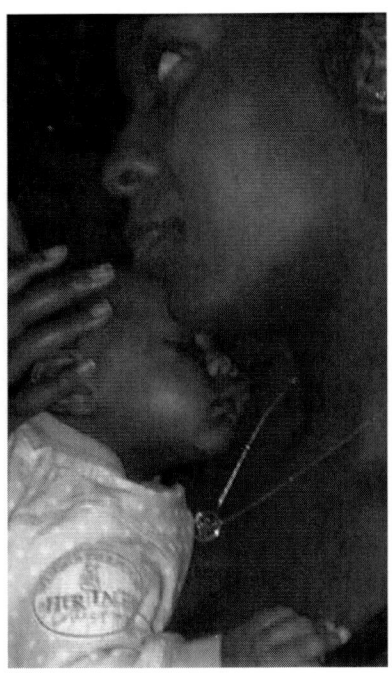
Malaika and her son Nosakhare

most notable and highly publicized name changes were those of Malcolm X and Mohammed Ali. On joining the Chicago Chapter of the Nation of Islam, Malcolm Little replaced his surname with an X to represent how enslavement robbed African people of their identity and cultural heritage. Fanon maintained that this loss produces 'individuals without an anchor, without horizon, colourless, stateless, rootless – a race of angels' (Fanon, 1968: 176). On his return from Mecca, Malcolm X again changed his name to El-Hajj Malik El-Shabazz.

Mohammed Ali, the world heavyweight boxing champion, said that his birth name 'Cassius Clay', lacked 'divine meaning': 'I am Muhammad Ali, a free name which means "beloved of God" – and I insist people use it when speaking to me.' 'Get used to me ... Black, confident, cocky – my name, not yours. My religion not yours. My goals, my own. Get used to me.'

Prior to his involvement with the Black Power movement and the struggle for the liberation of African people, Trinidadian born Stokely Carmichael described himself as someone who dated White girls and was 'the good little nigger' (Belton, 2007: 74). After his marriage to South African singer Miriam Makeba in 1969, Carmichael left America and went to live in Guinea, West Africa, changing his name to Kwame Touré in honour of the African leaders Kwame Nkrumah of Ghana and Sekou Touré of Guinea. Both leaders were known for being implacably opposed to Europe's colonization of Africa.

Following the broadcast of the television series *Roots*, based on Alex Haley's book, in 1977, Kizzy was the 17th most popular name given to African-American girls. Similarly, the name Marcus, in honour of Jamaican Pan-Africanist Marcus Garvey, was the 13th most popular name in the 1970s, and by 1983 was the fifth most popular name for African-American boys in Illinois. Playwright and poet Ntozake Shange changed her name from Paulette Williams in 1971. In Xhosa, Ntozake means 'she who has her own things', and in Zulu Shange is 'she/he who walks/lives with lions'. In her biography, Assata Olugba Shakur, a former political prisoner, wrote that 'the name JoAnne Deborah Byron Chesimard began to irk my nerves. I had changed a lot and moved to a different beat, felt like a different person. It sounded strange when people called me JoAnne'. In Yoruba, Assata means 'she who struggles', Olugba means 'for the love of the people' and Shakur, which means 'the thankful one', was the surname adopted in honour of Assata's friend Zayd Shakur (Belton, 2007: 125; Fitzpatrick, 2012: 67).

> In Africa, a name is considered to be very much part of the personality of the person. It is chosen with a great deal of care and consideration, often through divination ... It is believed that people assume the character, life and personality traits after whom they are named ... Among the Akan of Ghana a person has two names. The first name is the one he/she automatically assumes on the day they are born. This is the name of the day that they are born. The second name is a family name given to the child by the father.
>
> (Kirwen, 2008: 26)

The reclaiming of African names is not limited to African people in the Diaspora. Kamau wa Ngengi was the birth name of Jomo Kenyatta who, on the eve of Kenya's independence in 1963, became the country's first prime minister and in 1964 was elected the country's president. Kenyatta was among the Kenyans imprisoned by the British for alleged involvement in the Mau Mau struggle for land, freedom and self-governance (Maathai, 2007: 67). After his conversion to Christianity, Kenyatta had changed his birth name to that of John Peter. He later changed to Johnstone Kamau and then to Jomo Kenyatta. Ironically, this was not so in the case of South Africa's first Black president, whose Xhosa name Rolihlahla was changed by his teacher, Miss Mdigane, to Nelson (Fitzpatrick, 2012). The *Telegraph* article 'Nelson, Madiba, Tata – what's in a name?' (Alexander, 2013) suggested that the use of the clan name Madiba carried far more importance than Nelson's surname, Mandela. Peter Alegi, a specialist in South African history at Michigan State University, highlights the link between re-naming and colonialism: 'Using the Madiba name is to reclaim his African-ness and to downplay the Nelson part, which is a colonial legacy that unfortunately shackled much of the African continent for a long, long time' (Lee, 2013).

SANKOFA (ALSO KNOWN AS JUMOKE)

In the spirit of Sankofa, the traditional name Olajumoke Sankofa was bestowed upon me by Elder Lartey Addico. Olajumoke is a Yoruba name that means 'All wealth combined to pamper' the child. Ola literally refers to wealth, affluence or richness. Ju mo (combine effort, thoughts and plans), ke (pamper, treat well, spoilt child, shower the child with lots of love and affection). So Jumoke means: combined efforts shower her with love and affection. Sankofa is an Akan word that means 'We must go back and reclaim our past so we can move

Olajumoke Sankofa

forward so that we might understand who we are today'. We can reach back to take the best of what our past can teach us, so that we can fulfil our potential as we strive to go forward. Regardless of what we may have lost, forgotten or had stolen we can reclaim, revive, preserve and perpetuate. As a Diasporian Afrikan born and raised in Moss Side and growing up within the Abasindi family, the name Olajumoke Sankofa resonates with the heartbeat of Africa, reconnecting me to the authentic essence of who I am. It is a constant reminder of why I am here, and what I am here to do in service to my community, race and nation.

In his research on African-Caribbean family history, Guy Grannum outlined the difficulties faced by African-Caribbean people and the African Diaspora as a whole in tracing their ancestry and family history. According to Grannum, standard genealogical research in the UK relies on people having surnames that are passed on from father to child. After emancipation, freed men and women could also choose their own surnames or accepted names given to them by the church or the state. Although it was the practice in traditional African culture to have one or more personal names, it was uncommon for families to have a name that was handed down from generation to generation (Fitzpatrick, 2012). The assumption that parents were married before or soon after the birth of their first child does not reflect the reality of enslaved people. And their surnames were likely to be that of their last owner or former master or that of their mother or grandmother. During the period of enslavement, a man could be sold or transferred to another estate, leaving behind his children and their mother who, at a later date, might be sold without her children. In such a case it was customary for the slave owners to place the children in the care of the woman's mother (Henriques, 1960: 146). These women not only reclaimed the children but, as Walker says, 'more often than not [they] anonymously handed on the creative spark, the seed of the flowers they themselves never hoped to see' (Walker, 1983: 240) and in this way cultural knowledge was often transmitted. Issues of re-naming, re-claiming, culture and the creative spark of women came together in the role played by Abasindi women in the development of the Nia Centre for African and Caribbean Culture and Art.

Nia Centre

NIA CENTRE, CHICHESTER ROAD, HULME, MANCHESTER M15 5EU

During the 1980s the women of Abasindi were among the community groups and local people who became involved in the development of the Nia Cultural Centre, which was located in the former BBC Playhouse in Hulme.

The steering committee members and officers for the launch of the Centre in 1986/7 were Conway Mothobi, Pat Osborne, Keith Stephens, Elouise Edwards, Yasmin Hack, Lindford Sweeney, Tony Gordon, Trevor Plummer, John Lyons and Richard Davis. The Abasindi members on the committee were Abina Likoya, Yvonne Ahimie, Pauline Anguin, Yvonne Hypolite and Diana Watt. There was also Linford Sweeney, who was the leading founder member of Moss Side Arts Group, which had been established in 1982. The extract from the Moss Side Arts Group annual report 1983/4 stated that the Moss Side Arts Group (MAG) was formed in December 1982 by 'local members of the "Afro-Caribbean" community who strongly support the need for the development of Afro-Caribbean arts within the Moss Side area'. Alongside improving access in Moss Side to the best of African-Caribbean art forms, the group's long-term aim was the centralization of these activities in a suitably equipped single venue in or near Moss Side.

The implementation of these aims involved the regular promotion of events as well as the participation of both local and visiting artists. As a result MAG achieved a varied and balanced programme covering a wide range of art forms, namely dance, music, poetry and theatre. The promotion of events at different venues in and around Moss Side was an integral part of MAG's activities. Events took place at Birley High School, 8411 Community Education Centre, Abasindi Cooperative, the West Indian Sports and Social Club and the West Indian Centre in Carmoor Road (Bennett, 1987: 26).

The first event was held at Birley High School in Hulme on Sunday 20 March 1983 and featured two Liverpool-based artists, the poet Levi Tafari and Delado Dance and Drumming Group, which specialized in West African dance. During 1983 and 1984, local artists included Yootman Sound, poets Tshaka, Monique, Pat Berkeley and Keith Stephens and the Kantamanto Drumming Group led by Kwesi Asare. Kantamanto sought to give authentic expression to Ghana's traditional way of life, both in terms of spiritual development and ritual performances. Female vocalist Abina, whose repertoire embraces blues as well as contemporary and traditional songs from various countries in Africa, was also a regular performer. Abina and a member of Waduku who specialized in fusing traditional Ghanaian music, highlife and Afro Jazz.

An evening of poetry in April 1985 was organized in conjunction with Grass Roots Bookshop and Abasindi Cooperative. The event brought together women from different racial and cultural backgrounds. Abasindi dance and drumming workshops were held at the West Indian Centre Youth Club and 8411 Community Education and aimed to involve young people in the development and performances of various African-Caribbean art forms. In addition to local performers, international artists were featured such as the Jamaica National Dance Theatre and Sistren Theatre Collective. The performance by Sistren Theatre Collective was organized jointly by the women of Abasindi Cooperative and the organization War on Want, together with members of the Moss Side Arts Group. Over the last 37 years Sistren 'grass roots' Theatre Collective have been:

> ... educating working-class women about alternate ways to circumvent as well as dismantle the system that oppresses them economically, sexually and politically ... Of equal importance are the strong cultural links and pride in the indigenous culture that the group advocated. Sistren speaks the language of the masses and incorporated the folklore and songs of the islands into its theatre productions.
> (Davis and Ogundipe-Leslie, 1995: 34)

Sistren was established in 1977 by 13 women who lived in the poorest areas of Kingston, Jamaica. At the time the group's members were working as street sweepers as part of the Democratic Socialist Government Emergency Employment Programme for Unemployed Women – several later became teaching assistants. In the book *Lionheart Gal* Honor Ford-Smith, who was the group's artistic director for some years, argued that her work with Sistren represented 'an extension of her involvement in popular theatre and her belief in its importance for Caribbean identity' (Sistren Theatre Collective and Ford-Smith, 1986: iii). By way of drama, poetry, songs, music, dance, personal testimonies, oral history, rituals, role play and traditional ring games, Sistren addresses issues that adversely impact on the lives of Black working-class women. Sistren's first production, *Downpressure get a Blow*, focused on the struggles of garment workers to form a union. Lana Finiken, who has been a member of Sistren since it was established in 1977 and is the current Director, commented on the fact that the group's first production was the result of hours of group discussion and storytelling. The act of storytelling is concerned with issues of survival at two levels. It is about the survival of the storyteller who lives to tell the tale and the listener who has survived having learnt from the story (Nnaemeka, 1997: 7). Merle Collins, novelist and performance poet, observed that anyone seeing a Sistren performance would have the:

> Sensation of sharing in the lives of women who have been held within the grip of poverty, alienated by a brutal neo-colonial political system, brutalised by the police who also brutalise their

men, who in turn brutalise them. Their stories are those of women who have learnt to confront life with the same toughness with which it has confronted them, who want love and tenderness and caring but have learnt to carve a niche which ensures their survival in an unyielding atmosphere. Their experiences have given the strength and resilience which makes life possible even when it continues to be a constant struggle.

(Collins, 1988: 20)

Annette admiring craft work by Sistren Theatre Collective

The play *QPH* (1981), which Sistren performed at the 8411 Centre in Moss Side, was based on the lives of three women, Queenie, Pearlie and Hopie who had lived together at the Eventide Home for Destitute Women in Kingston, Jamaica. Pearlie died in 1979, and in 1980 more than 150 women, including Hopie, lost their lives in a fire that destroyed their 'home'. Although badly scarred, Queenie was among the survivors of the fire. In their exploration of the lives and aspirations of these women, both for themselves and their children, 'Sistren used the Etu ritual, a celebration for the dead through singing, dancing and feasting to tell the story. In that way, the production provided a space for participants to truly mourn the death of the women who were not projected as hapless destitutes but as our own companions on the journey of life' (Petromaxtheatre, 2006).

These cultural activities were taking place at a time when Moss Side was one of the wards described in a City Council report as 'characterised by high levels of unemployment, social deprivation and environmental decay'.

Cultural expressions of resilience

Following the disturbances in 1981, commonly known as the Moss Side riots (see Chapter 7), the Head of Personnel and Administration at BBC Manchester decided to vacate the premises they held in Hulme, which borders Moss Side, partially because of the fear that audiences might be reluctant to attend performances at the Hulme Playhouse. For members of the Nia Committee this was an opportunity to reverse negative perceptions of Moss Side. The Nia Centre planned a programme of music, visual and creative arts that would enhance the community's sense of pride and identity. This period coincided with the launch of the Arts Council of Great Britain Ethnic Minority Arts Action Plan in January 1986. The rationale for increasing funding for Black arts and spending a minimum of 4 per cent of its budget on the development of African-Caribbean and Asian arts was based on a number of factors, as outlined in the Council's 1985/6 annual report:

> The last two decades have seen a growth of arts activity amongst British people of Afro-Caribbean and Asian origin. African dancers and musicians have enjoyed an increased awareness and appreciation amongst audiences of all ages, artistic inclinations and ethnic origins ... Influenced by a consciousness of ancestral heritage and the immediate experience of life in contemporary Britain, these artists have developed a powerful voice which, heard and acknowledged, will have a profound and enriching influence upon the artistic life of our multi-cultural society.
>
> (Bennett, 1987: 14)

In the spirit of *Ujimaa* (which means collective work and responsibility), the aims of Moss Side Arts Group were consistent with those of the Nia Centre. The name Nia refers to one of the seven principles of Kwanzaa, an African festival that originated among the African-American community (Kwanzaa is also discussed in Chapter 4). Dr Maulena Karenga is the founder of Kwanzaa, which was first celebrated on 26 January 1966 in Los Angeles. Collectively, the seven core principles of Kwanzaa are referred to as the *Nguzo Saba*, a Swahili term. Beginning on 26 December, the celebration lasts for a period of seven days.

The Nia Committee perceived the history of Black art forms in England as one of exploitation and neglect. It was therefore important for Black people to develop a focus for their own culture and not rely on the efforts of others. This was in line with *Umoja*, the first principle of Kwanzaa, which represents unity, self-reliance and independence. It required self-determination and persistence, qualities that constitute the second principle: *Kujichagulia*. The relevance of the third principle, *Ujimaa*, was reflected in the letters of support from a number of organizations including the African Methodist Evangelical Church, Birley High School, Claremount Junior School, Churches Work Scheme, Central Area Community Education, Information Technology Centre, Family Advice and Community Resource Centre, West Indian Centre (WIOCC), Manchester Teacher's Centre, the Chief Constable and Members of Parliament. The fourth principle, *Ujamaa* (cooperative economics), and the fifth principle *Nia* (purpose) are celebrated within Kwanzaa on 30 December. This sense of 'purpose' and 'cooperative economics' was captured in the letter of support from the Family Advice Centre:

> As a Moss Side-based organisation, the Advice Centre has for many years been an advocate of the aims and objectives of the Nia Centre ... We are conscious that the absence of job prospects within the area of Moss Side has made it necessary for the inhabitants to create their own job market areas of music, art, dance and all aspects of cultural forms. Unhappily however, the area is devoid of the space and venues to enable the proper advancement of cultural activities and this has caused the cessation of a number of very promising groups and individuals who could have made a very positive contribution to music drama etc.

Drawing upon the sixth principle, *Kuumba* (creativity), the Nia Committee was committed to the development of an arts centre specializing in African-Caribbean culture. The Committee wanted a venue that was equipped to the highest professional standards and that would nurture, enhance and dignify the work of Black artists and would provide a creative space for young people and children in the community:

> What kind of people we become depends crucially on the stories we are nurtured on; which is why every sensible society takes pains to prepare its members for participation in its affairs by among other things, teaching them the best and the most instructive forms of its inheritance stories ... drawn from both the factual and the imaginative literature bequeathed by its ancestors: songs, poems, plays, epics, fables.
>
> (Riley, 2002: 247)

The seventh principle, *Imani* (faith), was a key component in the Nia Committee's determination to establish the centre. The group's unsuccessful attempt to acquire the Star Cinema on Withington Road, which was subsequently sold and later demolished, did not deter them from pursuing their ultimate goal. In commenting on the failure to acquire this building, Bennett (1987: 11) wrote, 'Although the objectives of the Nia Group have not yet been achieved, they have been tenaciously pursued over a two year period by a responsible group of people, clearly committed to seeing the Centre established and properly managed.'

Following the 1981 disturbances, the establishment of the Nia Cultural Centre was influenced by the work of men and women who were involved in the West Indian Overseas Coordinating Committee (WIOCC), Carmoor Road. Throughout its history in Manchester, the Centre had been at the forefront of promoting events that aimed to raise awareness of the educational and political struggles, and the cultural experiences and achievements of Black people, as expressed in its supplementary educational programmes, conferences, workshops and culture week celebrations. The annual Caribbean Carnival in Alexandra Park started in 1972 and the Roots Festival, involving collaborative work with local schools and community groups, got going. The Roots Festival not only placed emphasis on providing a platform for local children and young people to showcase their talents and ability, but was also committed to raising awareness about their cultural heritage. In its 1990/1 Annual Report, the Chairperson of the Nia Centre's Committee, Elouise Edwards, stated:

> The Nia Cultural Centre has begun a process of re-awakening our cultural traditions. For the first time in its history, this England has an African Cultural Centre of local, national and international fame. A Centre devoted to bringing together the talents and aspirations in art, theatre, music, dance, education etc., from people of different backgrounds and cultures. People who had been denied that opportunity – until now.

Artists that performed at the Nia Cultural Centre included Nina Simone, Gil Scott-Heron, The Mighty Sparrow, Uncle Tommy Odueso, Fela Kuti, Ziggy Marley, Gregory Isaac, Jean Binta Breeze, Baba Maal, Dennis Brown, Talawa Theatre Company, The Ghana National Company, Culture, Roaring Lion, Beres Hammond, Luke Dube and John Amos. Despite its determination to succeed, the organization's dependence on public funds, together with difficulties in translating the principle of cooperative economics (*Ujamaa*) into practical financing, meant that the centre was unable to sustain itself within the first five years, as was initially envisaged by the Nia Centre Committee.

THE RISE OF MANCHESTER'S NIA AFRICAN CULTURAL CENTRE
I became involved in the arts of my community as a teenager in 1973 when I was a member of what could have been the first Black youth theatre in Manchester, led by Prince Miller and operating out of Moss Side Youth Club. In 1976, I graduated to sitting on the Committee of MAAS NW (Minorities Arts North West), which had been established to develop and promote the arts and culture of minority ethnic communities living in the region. In 1979, while serving on the committee of MAAS NW, its Coordinator, Pnina Werbner, pointed out that African and Caribbean arts were not being sufficiently exposed to the North-West of England. We considered this to be a distinct and crucial gap in our cultural expression.

It was clear that there were no specific venues to showcase the richness of African and Caribbean arts. In addition, existing venues were inadequate and performances in traditional theatres and other venues did not reach such communities. For example, on the few occasions when African and Caribbean touring performers were funded and staged by traditional venues, the African and Caribbean communities would not become aware of ticket availability until the event had taken place. This situation led to a call by individuals within the communities for more accessibility, which the traditional venues found hard to answer owing to their lack of understanding about how to reach African and Caribbean communities.

At that time there were several Black-led arts groups in Manchester, including Kutamba (an African and Caribbean performance troupe led by Abina Likoya and consisting of dancers and drummers that toured the country from time to time), Black Kulture (my own youth theatre) and, later on, Kantamanto, led by Quasi Asare, an African percussion group. My own interest was stirred by the 1981 tour of the UK by the Black Theatre Cooperative, who performed at the West Indian Sports and Social Club. Although a venue within the community was used, it was wholly inadequate for staging professional theatre. Other venues had been suggested, such as the West Indian Centre in Carmoor Road and Abasindi. However, these venues were not properly equipped or even accessible enough to stage professional work.

It was clearly a frustrating time for the whole community, who wanted to attend more performances that spoke about and showcased their cultural backgrounds. And yet, in cities such as London, Liverpool and Birmingham these performances were taking place. After speaking with several people, Pnina suggested that I contact Abina Likoya at Abasindi to see whether anything could be done to rectify matters. At that time, Abasindi (formerly the Black Women's Cooperative) was the hub for many African and Caribbean arts and cultural activities in Manchester and had become a focal point for visitors, including artists, singers, dancers, musicians and more.

I approached Abina in 1982 and with several other people, including Diana Watt, Terry Brandy, Pauline Anguin, Shirley Gordon and Keith Stephens, we formed Moss Side Arts Group. Its initial brief was to provide access to touring African and Caribbean arts groups and companies and to identify an appropriate venue that could be developed to provide the professionalism and quality required to both house the arts and stage regular educational and cultural programmes of activities and events. We approached North West Arts for funding and they gave us £350.

Before Moss Side Arts Group was formed, several individuals and groups within the community had tried to initiate the development of a professional venue for the arts of African and Caribbean people. By 1983 the drive to obtain such a venue had become much stronger, with the Moss Side Arts Group regularly staging performances. Some events attracted up to 150 people. This meant that many different venues were used, and many of them were unsuitable. The emergence of the new group, led by Mrs Elouise Edwards, and including Richard Davis (Chair), Conway Mothobi, Quasi Asare, a host of young people and others created unity of expression and determination to find a solution to a growing problem. These meetings sometimes attracted up to 70 people and resulted in the establishment of the Nia African Cultural Centre, which I chaired for the first three years. Eventually Moss Side Arts Group became a part of this organization.

As Nia grew, it attracted more funds and its own full-time staff. Ervine Okuboh became its first Coordinator. Later, Alti Daniel became Nia's second Coordinator. The project was originally based at Abasindi. Eventually Nia became a limited company by guarantee and obtained charitable status, and we became the first Directors. Buildings were identified and feasibility studies were undertaken from around 1987, with the assistance of Judy Lancaster from MCCR, until a suitable building was located: the 'BBC building', as it was known, on Chichester Road in Hulme. This was a listed building, and had been in use as a hippodrome for many years until the BBC began using part of it as a rehearsal space for orchestras. The other half of the building had been used as a bingo hall. It was ideal. It boasted a 550-capacity theatre space, a large stage and room for expansion, and its location in the heart of the community suited everyone.

Around 1988, negotiations began to secure the 'BBC building' as the African and Caribbean communities' showcase venue of excellence. This was a long drawn-out process that included Manchester City Council and its Urban Fund, North West Arts Board (where I was first a panel member and then non-executive Director) and local residents. At that time we had the full support of North West Arts Board and their Community Officer, Liz Mayne, was instrumental in assisting us to manage the process of funding acquisition. Eventually, the project received £2.1 million from a combination of funding bodies and a seven-year lease. In 1989 refurbishments began to secure a badly damaged roof, and many internal changes were made, including a new reception area, offices, a kitchen, a spectacular skylight and a sturdier stage.

The Nia Cultural Centre opened in 1990, with a staff of about 20, including a Director (Morenga Bambata), an Events Manager (Alti Daniel) and several other managers, box office, kitchen and cleaning staff. At the time, it was considered to be the only project of its kind in Europe. The launch highlight was the appearance of Nina Simone! The African and Caribbean community were proud of the new facility and supported all its activities.

Linford Sweeney
African Heritage Historian and Author

The cultural work undertaken by Abasindi Black Women's Cooperative is akin to the role of their foremothers in ensuring the protection of African heritage. Significantly, Algerian feminist Awa Thiam argues that the survival of African customs was not an accident but instead resulted from the fruits of 'continual resistance', whereby the women in particular 'took it upon themselves to preserve certain customs' (Thiam, 1978: 123).

Protecting African heritage

It has been argued that a community can provide both space and opportunity for women to begin to determine and redefine its conditions (Williams, 1997). In their role as community and cultural activists, Abasindi Cooperative provided an important space for Black women to have their voices heard. Alice Walker's writings are concerned with rescuing Black women from silence through the establishment of sisterhood and 'womanist prose'. From a standpoint of resistance and resilience, the cultural work of Abasindi challenged the silencing of Black women and instead created a space for their involvement in wider struggles linked to the development of self and the community. The work of Abasindi and of the Nia Centre provided empowering spaces for Black arts to be used as a vehicle through which the community were able to play, celebrate achievements and resist the individual and collective experiences of oppressive practices.

Shirley Gordon

Chapter 4
Ancestral journeys and diasporic connections

Abasindi Pan-African Drummers and Dancers

A meeting of memory

One of the most visually dynamic elements of the Abasindi Cooperative was its dance and drumming group: the Abasindi Pan-African Drummers and Dancers (commonly known as the Abasindi Drummers and Dancers). The group was established shortly after the organization's inception but its legacy was to outlast it and even up to the time of writing, some years after the Cooperative ceased functioning, the group was often called upon to re-form for celebrations, funerals and community events. Like the organization itself, the Drumming and Dance Group was a loose and fluid collection of women who passed through, stayed or moved on from the group as the shape of their lives dictated. From initial tutelage by Nigerian Master Drummer, Thomas Odueso ('Uncle Tommy'), a legend in Manchester at the time, the women learned to play bongo drums, conga drums, the djembé, talking drums and percussive instruments.

Another local legend, Peddy, an expert in the creation of Carnival 'Mas' (Minshall, 2000) contributed to our knowledge of costume design skills, and from within came the talents for singing and dancing that we never knew we had. In the process, women found or reaffirmed an African heritage that enriched their lives:

Thomas Odueso ('Uncle Tommy')

> We learned many different dance styles from different parts of Africa ... from Ghana, Zimbabwe, South Africa ... I learned a lot about African culture through dance and song ... It was a place where I built my confidence up as well. It was kind of a journey, through developing myself.
>
> (Dahlia)

> I think Abasindi has made a tremendous impact on my life, it gave me the opportunity to meet so many people from all over the world really, and to travel. For my own personal development, I've always been interested in Arts ... meeting people from Africa gave me the opportunity to develop my skills in that area ... It's really enriched my life ...
>
> (Abina)
> (Interview extracts reproduced with permission from Schaffe, 2009)

Sometimes the group could count 12–15 voices for its performances, while at other times it comprised only 5 or 6. Over the years many women played the impressive array of traditional African instruments the Cooperative had acquired, and still more learned the dances passed on by visiting artists from Africa and the Caribbean. Abina, Diana, Pauline, Shirley May, Abiola, Moiwale, Dahlia, Kaya, Liz, Francia, Magdalene, Adele, Evadney, Lorraine, Tara, Sam, Caroline, Maria, Louise, Chalana, Miselo, Patricia, Esther, Emense, Mumba, Joy, Pauline, Madge, Joy Smith, Dorett, Shirley Gordon, Amina, Barbara, Merle and Estree were all performers with the group at one time or another, and there were others also.

Abasindi Dance Group

There were also children. Although professional drumming and dance performances were always performed by women, Abasindi ran workshops for children of the community, and those whose mothers were members of the group came to rehearsals and emulated our dance movements or joined the choruses to our songs. It was common to see a swollen-bellied woman in her seventh or eighth month of pregnancy wedged behind a bongo drum, and nothing soothed an Abasindi baby more than the steady drumming that is the heartbeat of any reggae rhythm or the South African Lullaby 'Thula Baba', which became one of the group's most popular songs:

African:
Thula thul', thula baba, thula sana,
Thul' ubab' uzofika, ekuseni. (repeat)
Kukhon' inkanyezi, eholel' ubaba,
Ekhanyisela indlel' eziy' ekhaya,
Sobe sikhona xa bonke beshoyo,
Bethi buyela ubuye le 'khaya,
Thula thula thula baba,
Thula thula thula sana,
Thula thula thula baba,
Thula thula thula sana.

English:
Keep quiet my child
Keep quiet my baby
Be quiet, daddy will be home by dawn
There's a star that will lead him home
The star will brighten his way home
The hills and stones are still the same my love
My life has changed, yes my life has changed
The children grow but you don't know my love
The children grew but you don't see them grow
> (Soweto Gospel Choir, www.metrolyrics.com/thula-baba-lyrics-soweto-gospel-choir.html)

MELANIE

Growing up, I remember there would be huge debates and many a raised voice in support of many causes. ... This would be followed by songs and music, reflected by a multitude of different African-Caribbean songs, sometimes accompanied by drumming.

My earliest memory to reflect this was marching and singing in a procession to demonstrate our pride: 'We are the children of mother Africa. You better clear the way let me pass.' With powerful mantras like these, as opposed to meaningless nursery rhymes, I felt connected with those who had come before me.

As a cooperative run on democratic and participative lines, the organization did not single out or acknowledge the role of leader as part of its structure. Nevertheless, one woman *does* stand apart for her singular contribution to the group and for promoting African music and dance in Britain more widely – Abina Likoya. Abina, one of the founder members of Abasindi and an accomplished jazz and blues singer and musician in her own right was the backbone of the group. During the 20 years when the Drummers and Dancers were most active, she was lead vocalist, lead drummer, designer and manager, organizing and directing the choreography, costume design and compositions for shows across the UK and Europe.

Relaxing in between gigs – on tour in Northern Ireland

Abina also took the group to Africa and the Caribbean, trips that evoked intense personal feelings and that cemented the Diasporic connections we discuss in this chapter.

Abina with some members of the group
From left to right: Kaya, Abina, Abiola, Lorraine, Francia

Reflecting on Abina's influence, Watt states:

> Within the group, this was indeed Abina's area of specialism and she can be counted amongst the people whom the Arts Council concluded were 'influenced by a consciousness of ancestral heritage and the immediate experience of life in contemporary Britain, these artists have developed a powerful voice which if heard and acknowledged, will have a profound and enriching influence upon the artistic life of our multi-cultural society'. Although Abina worked tirelessly to encourage the other women such as myself to move from a position of spectator to that of performer, initially I resisted in that I could not see the relationship between community activism and grass skirts ... However, my visit to Barbados to the Caribbean Festival of Arts (CARIFESTA) was a significant turning point in that the relationship between performer, spectators and audience were all interlinked. On our return to the UK ... the group agreed to establish the Abasindi drummers.
>
> (Watt, 2013: 72)

Abasindi was committed to promoting African and Caribbean culture and, in facilitating workshops in schools, colleges, community centres and other venues throughout Britain, the Drumming and Dance Group was one of the means of achieving this. But this was not the group's only role, or even its most important one. In this chapter we explore the political relevance of African dance in Britain during the 1970s and 1980s, and in examining some of the journeys undertaken by the group we unearth buried discourses of the function of dance and song within Black communities. For those whose recollections we have drawn on, this retrospective reflection represents a 'meeting of memory':

> We meet in the middle of memory
> Colliding against each other
> Like bats without radar
> Trying to find our way home
>
> Our voices are confused by languages
> That we are not always able to translate
> Yet we know the timbre of the sound our lips
> Vibrate upon

> Like drummers, we are masters of rhythm
> Beating a time of yesterday
> So that our spirits might soar on tomorrow
>
> We discover ourselves on continents south
> And even more southern
> On islands adrift from the mainland by centuries
> And remember the taste of our grandmothers cooking
> In pots we have never seen before
>
> Our rituals are not similar but the same
> Only the timing of dawn to dusk makes the difference
> Because our ancestors
> Once held hands in laughter
> Before the sorrow
> We are not trapped in memory
> We carry these memories inside of we
>
> What for you is history captured in a book
> sealed paint on canvas
> Is the nightly wail of terror
> That wets our eyes each morning
> And for a moment
> The mist of dawn is tinged with sorrow
>
> Anger is an ailment long ago pacified by endurance
> And the possibility that tomorrow
> Our ancestors will not simply be honoured
> But revenged
> So that the true history will be recorded
> For all our children to know
> And never let each or anyone of them enslave another
>
> **'REMEMBER we were AFRICANS before we were slaves'**
>
> ('Memory', SuAndi © 2007)

SuAndi reminds us to be cognizant of Africa's rich pre-slavery history. However, there is no doubt that slavery disrupted the dance form in irrevocable ways. If African dance was not political before slavery, then it certainly became so during it. The symbols and rituals of African dance and drumming became a source of resistance, communication and affirmation of identity among enslaved Black people that slave masters could not control and that have informed the development of dance in contemporary Caribbean societies to this day (Nettleford and LaYacona, 1985). Beckford and Levitt (2000: 13) points to the importance of the reworking and restoration of 'memory of the African and Caribbean past' to inform how we move forward, precisely the ethos that underpinned the work of the Jamaican National Dance Company that Nettleford and LaYacona wrote about.

Politics and culture are often discussed as though these are separate domains. They are not. The disparagement, distortion or misappropriation of cultural representations are politicized processes in so much as they contribute to hierarchies of oppression. Through dance we were reworking memory and affirming an aspect of African cultural heritage, which as Black women living and working in a society ridden with racism was itself a political act. As if to keep us on our political toes, Kath Locke, one of Abasindi's founders, would comment: 'always keep your culture political'. Our performances were infused with subliminal and overt messages about women's empowerment – what could be more political than that. For example, in our performances of the 1980s, we would often include 'Winnie', a song dedicated to Winnie Mandela's tireless struggle against apartheid. Later revelations about her involvement in the assault and kidnapping of a 14-year-old boy who was subsequently murdered were deeply disturbing, but at the time Winnie Mandela was emblematic of Black women's combined struggle against racism and gender oppression. The imprisonment she suffered and the enforced separation from her husband during his long imprisonment testified to the lives of many families who had been torn apart by apartheid and social injustice and we felt it important to remind people of the role of women in this political struggle (Qyason, 2014).

Given Abasindi's wider political goals it was unsurprising that the central narrative for *Ancestral Journey*, a production designed by the drummers and dancers and from which this chapter draws its title, was spun around Hetty, a Black slave from the former British colonies. We danced for Hetty as perhaps she once danced for her survival:

> African slaves, surreptitiously and openly, re-created an environment for their survival in the Caribbean, one in which their traditional belief systems were deeply planted. Dance, as non-verbal communication required no particular circumstances to reintroduce itself in the Caribbean and found regular expression as slaves celebrated birth, marriages, harvest, worship and death. In spite of the attempts by the governing nations to silence their

> cultural traditions, traditional religious rituals, music and dance seeped into everyday practices.
>
> (Ramdhanie, 2005: 84)

The chapter continues by describing the production and its meanings. We then discuss African dance within the context of British society in the 1980s and 1990s, and in the final section we describe the Abasindi Drummers and Dancers' performance at two iconic festivals, one in Africa and one in the Caribbean. These events are used to tease out the social significance of African music and dance in exploring Diasporic connections.

Hetty

The most significant production of the Abasindi Drumming and Dance Group was *Ancestral Journey* a dance drama developed in 1994, which, reflecting Beckford's point, aimed towards restoration of connections by linking the Diasporic experience to the historical legacy of slavery, but that also aimed to introduce the spectator to the tapestry of African dance, for which slavery was not necessarily a key reference point. Our programme read:

> Embracing the diversity of African women we travel the Ancestral journey. We remember and celebrate in ways handed down over generations ... Featuring songs and dances that originate from East, South and West Africa, the drummers and dancers add their own inimitable style and celebrate the survival and vitality of African peoples.

Hetty was a plantation slave in the British Caribbean colonies. She has no autonomous voice in the literature and we only know of her from a fellow slave, Mary Prince. Prince was 'freed/abandoned by her owners after she had travelled with them from Antigua to England' (Banner, 2013: 298) and was encouraged by abolitionists from whom she sought support to recount her story for publication. Prince claimed to represent not only her own voice but also the voices of other slaves – she asks that we take her account as authoritative: 'I have been a slave myself – I know what slaves feel – I can tell by myself what other slaves feel, and by what they have told me' (Prince, 1831 23). In her narrative Mary speaks for Hetty but it seemed that Hetty had also 'spoken' for Mary since her brutal treatment was to portend what was to come for Prince: one beaten-to-death slave simply replaced by another.

> The person I took the most notice of that night was a French Black called Hetty, whom my master took in privateering from another vessel, and made his slave. She was the most active woman I ever saw, and she was tasked to her utmost. A few minutes after my arrival she came in from milking the cows, and put the sweet-potatoes on for supper. She then fetched home the sheep, and penned them in the fold; drove home the cattle, and staked them about the pond side; fed and rubbed down my master's horse, and gave the hog and the fed cow their suppers; prepared the beds, and undressed the children, and laid them to sleep. I liked to look at her and watch all her doings, for hers was the only friendly face I had as yet seen, and I felt glad that she was there. She gave me my supper of potatoes and milk, and a blanket to sleep upon, which she spread for me in the passage before the door of Mrs. I——'s chamber.
>
> (Prince, 1831: 6)

The History of Mary Prince, A West Indian Slave, Related by Herself was published in 1831. This, the first account from a female Black slave woman from the British colonies, was one of several autobiographies of the time around which was spun an 'Enlightenment' discourse that linked the freeing of the slave with the acquisition of literacy (Larrabee, 2006: 454).

> The production of literature was taken to be the central arena in which persons of African descent could establish and redefine their status within the human community.
>
> (Henry Gates Jr. cited in Larrabee, 2006: 454)

Within a year of being published, *The History of Mary Prince* was into a third edition – its emotional weightiness considered a timely addition to the debate on the abolition of slavery (Deck, 1996). In 1833, two years after Prince's pamphlet came out, the Emancipation Bill was passed in the House of Lords, followed in 1834 by a law to establish apprenticeships for freed slaves in the 'British' Caribbean; in 1838 England abolished slavery in the Caribbean completely (Deck, 1996: 3).

Although Prince declares herself a 'more reliable authority on the subject than white men' (Deck, 1996: 3), the slave narratives of the eighteenth and nineteenth centuries were often considered incomplete unless accompanied by introductory or concluding text by a White person (often an abolitionist) that attested to the 'author's intellectual abilities and good moral character' (Banner, 2013: 298). The reliable authority of the voice of the slave, even the free slave, was considered, in itself, to be neither reliable nor authoritative. For credibility to be established it had to be corroborated: 'slavery's truth ostensibly made doubly true by the authenticating aid of a white voice' (Banner, 2013: 298).

In Mary Prince's account, Thomas Pringle, the Scottish abolitionist who helped her to publish her narrative, imposes his authority for establishing credibility so completely that, despite Prince's assertion, the control she exercises over her own voice is mediated through his greater power (Baumgartner cited in Banner, 2013: 298). Banner argues that in addition to the 'editorial infiltration' (298) of the abolitionist's voice, scholars have often overlaid their own meanings onto the stories told by slaves. Guided by the supposition that 'what the text means is what it does not say, which can then be used to rewrite the text in terms of a master code ... the [symptomatic] critic restores to the surface the deep history that the text represses' (Best and Marcus, 2009 in Banner, 2013: 298). Banner's work shows how these imposed voices stand in hierarchical relationship to the voice of the slave herself and reveal a 'racial power at work within the genre' (298). But if Mary Prince cannot even speak for Mary Prince, then who is to speak for Hetty?

Ancestral Journey invoked the notion of performative agency (Banner, 2013) through which the drummers and dancers provided a platform for the slave voice uninterrupted by overlaid meanings or White affirmation. The performance begins with a narrator delivering a slow-paced reading as Prince bears witness to Hetty's inhumane treatment and ultimate death. The narration is accompanied by continuous harmonic drumming – the drummers spontaneously break into explosive rhythm, beat a soulful or mournful melody or 'krrrakk ... krak ... krak' to reproduce the lash of the whip. All the while, the principle dancer moves free-form in response to the call of the drum or the voice, expressing what she feels in the moment.

> Poor Hetty, my fellow slave, was very kind to me, and I used to call her my Aunt; but she led a most miserable life, and her death was hastened (at least the slaves all believed and said so) by the dreadful chastisement she received from my master during her pregnancy. It happened as follows. One of the cows had dragged the rope away from the stake to which Hetty had fastened it, and got loose. My master flew into a terrible passion, and ordered the poor creature to be stripped quite naked, notwithstanding

her pregnancy, and to be tied up to a tree in the yard. He then flogged her as hard as he could lick, both with the whip and cow-skin, till she was all over streaming with blood. He rested, and then beat her again and again. Her shrieks were terrible. The consequence was that poor Hetty was brought to bed before her time, and was delivered after severe labour of a dead child. She appeared to recover after her confinement, so far that she was repeatedly flogged by both master and mistress afterwards; but her former strength never returned to her. Ere long her body and limbs swelled to a great size; and she lay on a mat in the kitchen, till the water burst out of her body and she died. All the slaves said that death was a good thing for poor Hetty; but I cried very much for her death. The manner of it filled me with horror. I could not bear to think about it; yet it was always present to my mind for many a day.

(Prince, 1831: 7)

In their interpretation, the Abasindi women who performed this scene were perhaps as guilty of over-layering meaning as are the scholars who study the genre of slave narrative. But there are some important differences. The first is that the interpretative power of performative agency was filtered through the experiential lens of Black women who felt a visceral connection to this ancestral heritage:

> Like drummers, we are masters of rhythm
> Beating a time of yesterday
> So that our spirits might soar on tomorrow
> (From 'Memory', SuAndi © 2007)

In contrast to the domination of cognitive forms of knowing (Larrabee, 2006), we believed the idiom of dance affirmed the agency of the spectator as much as the performer – what was knowable about Hetty's experiences was as much up to those who witnessed the performance as those who played it. A third difference is that we were part of the Abasindi Cooperative, informed by the everyday struggles of Black women of which we too were a part, a reality that sometimes left us depleted of energy but at other times infused us with determination.

Any dance drama that focuses on slavery is political. The slave trade is a highly politicized subject and this is nowhere more keenly evident than in the intention of Caribbean governments to seek reparations from the former European slave-trading nations (the UK, France, Spain, Portugal, the Netherlands, Norway, Sweden and Denmark). In March 2014 heads of state from 15 Caribbean countries unveiled a plan demanding reparations from Europe that aims to achieve 'justice for the people who continue to suffer harm at so many levels of social life' (Sir Hilary Beckles, Chair of the Reparations Commission, quoted in Pilkington, 2014). One of the most important demands of the plan is for 'European countries to issue an unqualified apology for what they did in shipping millions of men, women and children from Africa to the Caribbean and America in the 17th and 18th centuries' (Pilkington, 2014). Other reparations called for include:

- diplomatic help to persuade countries such as Ghana and Ethiopia to offer citizenship to the children of people from the Caribbean who 'return' to Africa
- a development strategy to help improve the lives of poor communities in the Caribbean still devastated by the after-effects of slavery
- cultural exchanges between the Caribbean and West Africa to help Caribbean people of African descent rebuild their sense of history and identity
- literacy drives to improve education levels in Caribbean communities where this is needed
- medical assistance to a region struggling with high levels of chronic diseases such as hypertension and type 2 diabetes that have been linked to the fallout from slavery.

Although outside the scope of this chapter, one of the challenges for the reparation movement is how to address the role of African nations in this trade. Slavery in West Africa preceded and outlasted the Atlantic slave trade, existed alongside it and oiled its machinery (Schramm, 2007; Kankpeyeng, 2009), and as Schramm states: 'In royal armies and courts as well as in agriculture, slaves constituted a major workforce' (Schramm, 2007: 71). Domestic slavery and trans-Saharan slavery continued in West Africa for more than a hundred years after the abolition of slavery in Britain and was only outlawed in 1928 with the institution of the Abolition of Slavery Ordinance (Kankpeyeng, 2009: 209). The prevalence of slavery in Africa before the Atlantic trade made ready accomplices for the Europeans among those who had already established systems of domination. Slavery clearly has a complex history but few would disagree that the trans-Atlantic slave trade, which went on for more than 300 years, was particularly brutal, resulted in mass dislocation and genocide and has had more profound global ramifications at social, economic and political levels than any other historical event (Schramm, 2007: 71). Relevant to Abasindi's production of *Ancestral Journey* is Beckles's observation that the symbolism of acknowledgement and apology for the costs of the trans-Atlantic slave trade play an important part in the restoration of human dignity and human rights. Beckles observes that: 'America has made efforts to reflect on their own history, but Britain has made no such effort to do so. If the British public were shown slavery in their own society seen through the eyes of the enslaved, they would get a much better understanding' (Pilkington, 2014). Abasindi's *Ancestral Journey* was an attempt to do just that – to portray slavery in British society through the eyes of the enslaved.

There were more opaque meanings as well. Drumming and dance were used by slaves to communicate through a language not accessible to their masters, though prohibitions and punishments for doing so were severe. There was an irony in using African dance and drumming to foreground slavery when slaves had been brutalized when they danced for themselves and brutalized to make them dance for the master. As Lynne Fauley Emery wrote in *Black Dance: From 1619 to today*:

> The African was forced to dance in bondage and under the lash. He danced because the White ruler wanted his stock in good condition. He danced not for love, nor joy, nor religious celebration or event, or to pass the time; he danced in answer to the whip. He danced for survival.
>
> (cited in Ramdhanie, 2005: 78)

The trans-Atlantic slave trade represents a traumatic interruption in the evolution of African societies and had enduring effects. In marking its abolition *Ancestral Journey* included emancipation songs from the Caribbean. Emancipation Day was first celebrated in the former British colonies of the Caribbean on 1 August 1834, a year after the 1833 Abolition of Slavery Act, and continues to be observed widely in the region and in parts of Africa. Slavery is not, however, the whole of Africa's story and in traditional African dance is not a defining factor at all because the meanings and function of dance have long existed outside of this context. For this reason *Ancestral Journey* also showcased dances and songs from different regions of Africa. The varied dances included those reflecting war and resistance, courtship, play and celebration and though largely based on traditional dance, the movements were interpreted through the perspectives of Black women from the UK whose lineage to Africa was far from straightforward.

Diana Watt and Adele D. Jones

The politics of African dance

Larrabee (2006) deconstructs the narrative of Mary Prince in order to critique what she calls the 'standard' epistemological viewpoint. She draws on an extensive body of feminist literature to challenge the logocentric dominance of cognitive forms of knowledge that place the mind in 'dichotomous relation' to the body and that, she suggests, present the subject 'as too narrow, as disembodied, as "autonomous" and therefore non-social' (Larrabee, 2006: 456). From Abasindi's viewpoint, the meshing of dance, drumming *and* political activism was a means of achieving the 'embodied and culturally adumbrated' knowledge for which Larrabee argued. Drumming and dancing gave us the opportunity to express our representations of socially significant but invisible events, and though there was often opacity to our performances we also validated literal, surface meanings; our target was not the 'rational' subject but the social being.

In Hetty, through the storytelling of Mary Prince, we connected ourselves as Black women to a long line of female ancestors who had faced and fought racialized and gendered subjugation. Though the trans-Atlantic slave trade was history, contemporary life in the UK was fraught for many Black women, as other chapters in this book show. The drumming, drama and dance in *Ancestral Journey* were means of weaving history into these contemporary realities. The 'knowledge' produced through our performance was not easily categorized. For the performers, learning was internalized – this was about discovery, self, identity, place, belonging and connectedness; performing to Mary Prince's narrative about Hetty was intensely moving and we were deeply affected. What the spectator gained, only the spectator can say, but our aim was to showcase drumming and dancing as a vital aspect of African and Caribbean culture, not as reified or fossilized artefact but as a dynamic, organic art form that has history, social context and contemporary relevance.

We had learned traditional African dances from visiting artists and professional dancers/choreographers, people such as Peter Badejo and George Dzikunu (of Adzido Dance Company). These men were among the most influential promoters of African dance in the UK, but our interpretation of the dances were inevitably filtered by our Diasporic experiences and were anything but traditional. For example, the Zulu war dance taken out of its South African context could only claim a loose connection to the history of Kwa-Zulu-Natal, but as a symbol of resistance and agency it could not have spoken more loudly of that connection.

Ancestral journeys and diasporic connections

Abasindi Drummers and Dancers – Zulu War Dance
From left to right: Emense, Evadney, Mumba, Abiola (drums), Magdalene, Adele, Estree – Abina, Liz, Francia and Kaya (drummers) are hidden from view

If this was indeed traditional dance, then we were rewriting history because all these 'warriors' were women. But this was not history rewritten and neither was it parody – we used African dance to symbolize the role of Black women at the forefront of struggle within a specific socio-historical context, while at the same time passing on 'culturally adumbrated' knowledge; or so we hoped. Beyond mere entertainment, the strength and determination we sought to convey through dance were unequivocal and when the drumming called the warrior to raise up and stamp the ground, the message 'come no closer, you don't know who you are dealing with' seemed more resonant of everyday life than of the preservation of tradition. As Magdalene (third from the right in the photograph) danced solo – body taut, crouched low and spear held high, her eyes daring her potential violator to cross the line – it was electrifying. We danced for others but clearly we also danced for ourselves – the affirmation of Black history, culture, identity and womanhood interlocking in one to locate the self:

> I was brought up with a Black father and a White mother; I had no influence from Black women, at all. As I got older, I felt kind of like quite isolated and then when I started to get involved in Abasindi, it was like I'd found my Black women.
> (Liz)
>
> (Interview extract reproduced with permission from Schaffe, 2009)

This book is the only text to comprehensively document the role of the Abasindi Cooperative in Black women's activism and though several references to the Abasindi Drummers and Dancers can be found (see for example Ramdhanie, 2005), the group did not conform to any attempts to classify it. In Ramdhanie's impressive thesis, he mistakenly classifies the Abasindi Dancers and Drummers as a traditional African dance group:

> [Traditional African Dance] TAD refers to practice that maintains its repertoire when it is transferred from traditional African communities to performance spaces 'outside' of this setting. For instance, a dancer in England researches and re-presents a dance that he/she has practiced or observed on the continent. The dancer expresses creativity in reproducing the traditional form through the execution of floor patterns. In this sense he/she is not a choreographer but a 'dance arranger' of traditional dance practice. The presentation maintains its 'narrative' and provides a context of a particular community. This maintains the traditional form in the Diaspora and ensures that besides the exactitude of the vocabulary in terms of gestures and symbols, costuming, musical accompaniment, religious and spiritual invocations, the forms provide continuity, meaning and a 'reaffirmation of self' for various Black communities in the Diaspora. Adzido Pan-African Dance Ensemble, AfiDance, ADANTA and Abasindi Dancers and Drummers etc., most notably mirror the TAD movement in England.
>
> (Ramdhanie, 2005: 24)

There are hundreds, possibly thousands, of traditional African dances. It is important that the movements and gestures of some dances are preserved because, as with changing a word in an oral language, changing a gesture can change meaning. However other dances might permit a degree of improvisation and modification, depending upon the age, kinship and status of the performer (Welsh, 2004). Traditional dance in African societies is an integral part of everyday life. Used to mimic, mark or celebrate the ordinary as well as the exceptional, it accompanies birth, death, work and play, is a medium for the transmission of social values and enables people to encounter the gods they wish to appease or worship (Welsh, 2004). Traditional dance is also about relationships and is often segregated by gender, reinforcing gender boundaries and roles. Both men and women dance (often separately) but in most traditional dances it is the men who provide the drumming. The

Abasindi drummers were all women – figuratively the women of the group were foundation, keystone and castle:

> I always admire drummers ... the fact that they are the mainstay, they still keep going no matter what.
>
> (Francia, drummer and dancer)

The rebuttal of the imposition of the woman's place implicit in the term 'traditional' that was signified by women taking up the drum suggests this was a political position. It was. It was also joyously empowering. On several occasions Abasindi drummers were invited on stage to perform with other bands; the skill of the women in keeping pace with accomplished male drummers engendered mutual respect that was seldom evident otherwise. Spectators familiar with West African dance and music were sometimes astonished to see the proficiency of our drummers on the djembé, as this instrument is rarely played by women (Flaig, 2010).

Our distancing from the term 'traditional' was also based on deep respect for the religious connections of some dances in African societies (see for example, Turner's 1968 text *Drums of Affliction*; Euba (1992) on drumming for Yoruba religious rites; Dargie (1992) *Musical Practices of the Xhosa People* and Impey, 1998). As a secular organization encompassing faith-holding and non-faith-holding women alike, we did not seek to promote the religious meanings of any of the songs we sang. Being non-traditional was an important creative standpoint too, as the Abasindi Drummers and Dancers operated from a pluralistic, rather than dualistic position that embraced the cross-pollination of African and Caribbean cultural modes of expression.

But if we did not represent traditional African dance, we could not be classified as a contemporary Black dance troupe either. We learned traditional African dances but danced them in our contemporary realities that for us, as women of the African and Caribbean Diaspora, were loaded with multiple, often contradictory, meanings. For example, we were as comfortable dancing a modest courtship dance of the Luo people of Kenya as we were spicing up the dance by throwing in a 'wine' (a contemporary Caribbean dance movement that involves an emphatically sexualized gyration of the hips, usually danced to calypso and soca music).

Though we appreciated the importance of the cultural, spiritual and social meanings of the dances we learned, we were outsiders to their nuanced contexts. We did not re-present or 'arrange' dances we had learned on the continent of Africa and, on the contrary, visitors from Ghana, Nigeria, Sierra Leone, Zimbabwe, Kenya, Uganda and South Africa brought the continent

Abasindi dancers

to us. Though we kept dances true to their original form where we could, being performed by Black women in Britain, outside their historical and social locations meant they melded with other influences and became something else. The ambiguity and hybridization we created we thought worthy of celebration, although traditional dance purists must have shaken their heads in dismay. That this hybridization was as apparent in our costumes as in our dances can be seen in the photograph: the hats take their shape from those worn by the Zulu women of South Africa, while the dancers' manipulation of the long flowing skirts is reminiscent of the quadrille dress, the folk costume of the Caribbean.

The social and political context in which the Abasindi Drummers and Dancers performed was informed by the wider Black Power and anti-racist activism that emerged during the 1970s and 1980s in Britain. The resurgence in the celebration and reclaiming of African and Caribbean culture, of which dance was a part, is described by Ramdhanie (2005: 36, citing Fielding Stewart) as 'Black resistance in the social, political and personal realms'. Black dance or 'African Peoples' Dance', defined as that 'which draws its main influence, sensitivities, means of experience and technical base from the cultural heritage of Africa and the peoples of Africa living in the Diaspora' (Irie Dance Theatre, 2014) enabled young Black people in Britain to forge connections with the Caribbean and Africa (Ramdhanie, 2005).

Although Caribbean and African dance forms are connected, they have different evolutionary paths. Caribbean dance has inevitably been shaped by trans-Atlantic slave routes, incorporating different influences along the way and often signalling covert messages of resistance. Ramdhanie (2005: 27) writes about religious practices in the 'New World': 'Sango in Trinidad and Tobago, Kumina in Jamaica, Santeria in Cuba, Voodoo in Haiti [and] Candombli in Brazil'. He describes the ways in which the African dance forms that accompanied these belief systems were suppressed and their followers punished. Yet slavery is not a key anchor point for traditional African dance and although undoubtedly infected by colonial encounters, it is not defined by them (Adair and Burt, 2013). These different but connected histories are reflected in the development of Black dance in the UK.

The first Black dance company in Britain, Ballets Nègres was founded in 1939 by a Jamaican man who was taught to dance by the Maroons, the descendants of runaway slaves (V&A, 2015). Other dance companies influenced by Caribbean heritage include the Delado Dance and Drumming Company founded in Liverpool in 1981 (Rogers and Gallagher, 2006) and the Phoenix Dance Company, founded in 1982. The Phoenix Dance Company, one of the most successful companies in the UK, was established by three young men from Leeds: Leo Hamilton, Donald Edwards and Villmore James who, though refusing to be compartmentalized as 'Black dance', gained much of their inspiration from the narratives of the migration of Caribbean elders to Britain (Kruczkowska, 2007; Association of Dance of the African Diaspora, 2013a). Dance companies in operation at around the same time as the Abasindi Dancers and Drummers included Irie Dance Theatre in London (founded by Beverley Glean in 1984 and still in existence); Kantamantu in Manchester; Lanzel in Wolverhampton; Sankofa in Birmingham and Ekome in Bristol (Association of Dance of the African Diaspora, 2013b). (For a short summary of the history of Black dance in Britain from the 1940s to the present see Adair and Burt, 2013).

What set Abasindi apart from these groups is that we were never a professional dance company. We represented the cultural arm of a Black women's organization that was engaged in serious political struggle against racism and gender oppression, issues that informed the songs we sang and our decisions about self-representation. For example, we were active supporters of the anti-apartheid movement and often concluded our sets with 'Nkosi Sikelel' iAfrika', the South African national anthem (then the ANC anthem) and only ceased doing so when Nelson Mandela was released from prison. We were volunteers, who squeezed rehearsal time in between jobs, study and childcare, and any Black woman could join the group regardless of talent or skill. The high standards we achieved, evident in numerous bookings for festivals and concerts, were due to our abundant enthusiasm and the dedication of the group's leader Abina, who refused to settle for mediocrity. Although there were many highlights, up there at the top was the time we supported Ladysmith Black Mambazo at the Apollo Theatre in Manchester in the late 1990s. Another memorable performance was at the National Theatre in Accra, Ghana as part of the Pan-African music festival, PANAFEST.

Diana Watt and Adele D. Jones

African dance has made a significant contribution to dance in Britain for over 75 years (www.adad.org.uk; V&A, 2015), however it was no coincidence that Black dance groups burgeoned in the late 1970s and early 1980s. Set against a backdrop of the upsurge in Black political awareness and the reclamation of an African heritage following decades of disparagement and marginalization, African and Caribbean culture provided a peaceful means of challenging racist representations. As Ramdhanie states, 'Psychologically, there was a new awakening in the definition of "self" and an increased awareness and spiritual connectivity between Black people in the Caribbean, Africa and in the New World generally (Ramdhanie, 2005: 31). This was a period marked by mass protests and riots against racial and economic disadvantage (see Chapter 7). Some people took to the streets for racial equality while others danced for racial pride – different coordinates on a shared political landscape.

Abasindi Dancers and Drummers performed at all kinds of events but its purpose within the local Black communities of inner-city Manchester was to embed African music within everyday social life in much the same way as in Africa. We danced and drummed for naming ceremonies, for Kwanzaa[1], as part of carnival celebrations, for weddings, wakes, funerals, social gatherings and for Black History Month. We opened conferences and we closed them. We were present to mark the milestones of many Black organizations, for instance we were part of the rituals for the land-turning ceremony when the Bibini Centre was built (Jones and Waul, 2005), at the opening of the Kath Locke Centre (www.kathlockecentre.co.uk) and at numerous events held by the West Indian Community Centres. For many years, we were a regular feature at International Women's Day celebrations, we performed at charity events, anti-deportation campaigns and anti-apartheid concerts, and when one of the Abasindi women was appointed a university professor, we shook up the hallowed halls of that academic institution when we drummed at her inaugural lecture.

In the next section we reflect on the significance of our Diasporic connections, cemented through two of the festivals at which we performed: the Pan-African Festival of Music (PANAFEST) in Ghana and the Crop Over Festival in Barbados.

Diasporic connections

PANAFEST is a festival of African dance and music held in Ghana every two years. Building on Ghana's unique contribution to the politics of African independence, the festival aims include the promotion of Pan-Africanism and the development of the African continent.

The origins of Pan-Africanism lie in the slave rebellions and resistance of the nineteenth century (Abdul-Raheem, 1996) but the term seems to have first surfaced in 1900 when Trinidadian barrister Henry Sylvester Williams called a conference to challenge racial discrimination and British colonialism (Abdul-Raheem, 1996). Pan-Africanism was initially led by scholars from the Diaspora, most notable among them being W.E.B Du Bois, who convened the first Pan-African Congress in Paris in 1919. Further congresses followed, each building on the scholarship and theory of Pan-Africanism: 1921 (London, Brussels and Paris), 1923 (London and Lisbon) and 1927 (New York), with the most significant being the fifth Congress, held in Manchester in 1945. Ghanaian statesman Kwame Nkrumah was one of the key organizers, and in 1957 he led Ghana to independence from Britain. The Manchester Congress was the first to include a large number of Africans from the continent and is credited with providing 'impetus and momentum for the numerous post-war independence movements' (Pan-African Development Education and Advocacy Programme, n.d.). Woven throughout the political narrative of Pan-Africanism were intellectual discourses and cultural developments including: 'the Harlem Renaissance, Francophone philosophies of Negritude, Afrocentrism, Rastafarianism and Hip Hop ... [while] Post-independence, a new generation of African writers – such as Chinua Achebe, Wole Soyinka, Bessie Head gave voice to issues that could be recognised throughout the Continent' (Pan-African Development Education and Advocacy Programme, n.d.).

Pan-Africanism is not without its detractors. It is often criticized for an over-simplified analysis of causal and contributory factors to Africa's underdevelopment, and scholars such as Obadina (1997) have drawn attention to the need for African nationalists to examine some of the internal constraints to progress:

> African ruling elites who have pillaged their people's wealth and held their nation's development to ransom are more culpable than Pan-Africanists acknowledge.
>
> (Obadina, 1997: 316)

Perhaps one of the most important issues to blight the Pan-Africanist movement is its relative silence on the subordination of women and its failure to tackle patriarchal domination: 'The conditions which determine the African woman's state are imposed on her by a society which maintains rigid social-cultural values and practices against her' (Obadina, 1997: 316). That the most significant Pan-African Congress should have taken place in Manchester, the birthplace of the Abasindi Cooperative, which was committed to ending women's subordination, is more than a symbolic link. The founders of Abasindi may have been influenced by Pan-Africanist thought but they were fiercely determined to ensure that women's liberation was stamped indelibly on any causes it supported. As we discuss elsewhere in this book, Abasindi grew out of the upsurge of activism against racial inequality and the celebration of Black pride that took place in the 1970s, mass movements that were sweeping the Diaspora. Pan-Africanism was reignited by this groundswell of popular action in a way that is unlikely to have been achieved by politicians or scholars alone, and within the small circles in which Abasindi operated, we pushed against its gender barriers in many ways, including through the Drumming and Dance Group.

Despite its limitations, Pan-Africanism remains an important force for political and academic debate and a vital platform for the cross-pollination of cultural ideas (Pan-African Development Education and Advocacy Programme, n.d.). As if to emphasize this, PANAFEST 2013, which coincided with the 50th birthday of the African Union (AU, formerly the OAU) and the 50th anniversary of the death of W.E.B Du Bois, included several activities focused on the theme 'Pan-Africanism and the African Renaissance' (www.ghana.travel/events/panafest/). PANAFEST is also concerned with the re-memorying of slavery (beyond remembrance and somewhere between history and imagination, we use the term 're-memorying' to symbolize a reflective process that seeks to connect the person to the history of slavery). Ghana served as a vital link in the trans-Atlantic slave trade and an estimated 12 million Africans are said to have been shipped to America and the Caribbean from the European forts and castles that dominate its coastal landscape:

> These forts and castles were designated as national monuments in 1972, and in 1979 the forts of Elmina and Cape Coast were inscribed on the UNESCO World Heritage list for their historic role in European–African interactions and the emergence of the globalised world.
>
> (Kankpeyeng, 2009: 209)

Diasporic Africans regard the slave forts of Elmina and Cape Coast as centres for spiritual veneration and their role as tourist sites have become a vital source of foreign exchange for the Ghanaian economy. One main event of the PANAFEST festival is a pilgrimage along the UNESCO-sponsored Slave Route.

The Abasindi Drummers and Dancers participated in the PANAFEST festival of 1995; our 12-day tour enabled us to travel to different parts of

Ghana conducting workshops, performing and taking part in jamming sessions with artists from around the world. One of the main performances took place at Elmina Castle, possibly the most widely known slave fort in the world. We spent the day there before our performance that evening; it was an emotionally charged experience for us all. The physical structure of the castle, with the ocean crashing against its walls, is all the imagination needs to be transported to the herding of slaves within its walls. No artificial tricks or tourist trappings could do this – it really is the place itself. Its feet-thick walls and iron grilles exude utter misery. We wandered first as a group, becoming quieter and quieter – until we were almost silent. Then we drifted apart, each of us sinking into ourselves. It was impossible to escape our own thoughts; this was our history, we were connected to it in ways that recalled Hetty.

Twenty years later, as we write this book, the memories are still vivid: we see the sun glistening from the metal of the ball and chain, polished to a high shine by thousands of visitors; the balcony above the women's pen from which the White slave trader would pick his rape victim for the night, and the exit passageway that led from the castle to the ocean and the waiting ships. This last detail is perhaps the most distressing of all: the passageway had been narrowed so as to allow only one person at a time to exit. When first built, it had been wide so as to speed up the processing of transportation, but hundreds of slaves leapt from the ledge to their deaths, preferring to drown in the ocean than to endure as slaves. The traders could not afford this loss of 'property' and found it easier to prevent suicide by narrowing the gap. Our performance that night was possibly one of our best: we danced for our ancestors but afterwards we talked until the early hours to rid ourselves of sadness:

> What for you is history captured in a book,
> sealed paint on canvas
> Is the nightly wail of terror
> That wets our eyes each morning
> And for a moment
> The mist of dawn is tinged with sorrow
>
> (From 'Memory', SuAndi © 2007)

If the Elmina performance had been emotional, the fact that we were billed to perform at the National Theatre in Accra as part of the festival's finale was frankly intimidating. Ghana's National Theatre was built in 1990. Seating 1,500 people in the main auditorium, the theatre is home to the National Dance Company, the National Symphony Orchestra and the National Theatre Players. Anyone who has seen the National Dance Company of

Ghana perform will understand our trepidation. Established in 1962 from artistic developments initiated by Kwame Nkrumah, the first President of the Republic of Ghana, the company, then with about 60 performers, had toured the world to rave reviews (National Commission on Culture, 2006). It was not only the incredible skill of the performers that daunted us; F. Nii-Yartey, who had been Artistic Director of the company since 1976, was well-known among the African dance circles in Britain in the 1980s and was credited as being the inspiration behind many of the groups mentioned earlier. The Abasindi Drummers and Dancers were a community group and only Abina, who was a popular jazz singer in Manchester, could be described as a professional performer; the rest of us made our living doing other things.

We had fielded a group of 12 women but needed to fill a stage that was at least 60 feet across; our 12-foot-square backcloth – a beautiful batik tapestry created by a Sierra Leonean artist – seemed insignificant and was instantly lost against the back curtain. We felt under-skilled and overwhelmed. We should not have worried – our hosts were more than gracious. Our set was received with rapturous applause and the performers of the National Dance Ensemble all rose to give us a standing ovation. Our performance was not comparable with theirs, not in the slightest – this was immediately apparent when they took the stage. But we, a small group of women from an unknown community in Manchester, had given our all, and the appreciation was palpable.

The second most significant of Abasindi's Diasporic connections was in Barbados, most notably the Crop Over Festival. In Barbados, Emancipation Day is part of the annual 'Season of Emancipation', which includes the anniversary of the 1816 Slave Rebellion led by Bussa (a national hero), the International Day for the Remembrance of the Slave Trade and its Abolition and the Crop Over Festival. Crop Over, Barbados is one of several indigenous carnival festivals in the Caribbean. These differ from music festivals in that as well as music and dance, they include masquerade and other performing arts. During slavery, crop over festivals were common across the region, marking the end of the sugar-cane harvest. Barbados was the Caribbean's largest sugar producer and Crop Over was a particularly significant event. The earliest reference to the festival in Barbados was in 1788, when the manager of Newton Plantation wrote to inform the estate's owner in England that he had held a 'dinner and sober dance' for the slaves, saying: "twas a celebration of Harvest Time after the crop' (www.funbarbados.com/crop_over/history.cfm).

Crop Over provided an opportunity for the resurgence of African music and dance and was considered an indicator of the enslaved African's spirit of indomitability (Beckles, 2002). A major concern among slave owners at the time was that free time and socialization bred rebellion. They were not wrong, but crop over festivals persisted (Beckles, 2002). After the abolition of slavery, plantation life continued and the festival remained an important marker on the calendar. By 1940, however, the sugar industry had begun to decline and other sources of employment were developing. The end of plantation life brought an end to the festival. In 1974, Crop Over, Barbados was revived to boost tourism and today it bears little relation to the festival during the time of slavery. Nevertheless there are still historical remnants, although these are only symbolic. The festival lasts for five weeks, beginning with the 'Ceremonial Delivery of the Last Canes' and the crowning of the King and Queen of the Festival – the 'most productive male and female cane cutters of the season'. Crop Over is regarded as an 'extravaganza of music and masquerade, history and culture' and is a major feature on the regional tourism calendar:

> The grand finale is the *Grand Kadooment*! This carnival parade features large bands with 'revellers' dressed in elaborate costumes to depict various themes. Designers of these bands compete for the coveted Designer of the Year prize while the revellers seem more intent on having a good time! The revellers make their way from the National Stadium to Spring Garden accompanied by the pulsating rhythm of calypso music. When they reach Spring Garden, the party continues with more fantastic music, lots of food and drink and, for some, a quick swim at the nearby beach. A grand end to a grand festival.
>
> (www.funbarbados.com/crop_over/history.cfm)

In the early 1990s, the Abasindi Dancers and Drummers travelled to Barbados to perform in several of the concerts given during the festival. In Ghana we had felt 'Like bats without radar, trying to find our way home' but Barbados reminded us that 'our ancestors once held hands in laughter' ('Memory', SuAndi © 2007). If PANAFEST was homecoming, Crop Over was liberation and abandonment. The group was privileged to perform in programmes and workshops that also featured Pinelands Creative Workshop, who specialize in carnival arts, and with Dancing Africa, Barbados's own celebrated African Dance Company. We swam in the beautiful seas of the South Coast and participated in the festival parades. Ghana had brought back reflections of slavery but we were 'not trapped in memory' and in Barbados we celebrated the emancipation of Hetty and other enslaved foremothers.

The Abasindi Drumming and Dance Group was a vehicle for rediscovering the value of African and Caribbean cultural heritage – our journey was historical, political and personal and though we shared everything we learned along the way, the greatest beneficiaries of our Ancestral Journey were ourselves.

Endnotes
[1] Kwanzaa takes its name from a Swahili phrase 'matunda ya kwanza', which means 'first fruits of the harvest'. The seven-day end-of-year holiday was established in 1966 in the US by Maulana Karenga to celebrate African heritage. It has been adopted by several Black communities in the UK and Europe (www.history.com/topics/holidays/kwanzaa-history).

Chapter 5
Loving body, skin and hair

'Ain't I a woman ...?' Not so much a question as an exclamation, this famous phrase, the axis around which Sojourner Truth constructed the speech she presented at a women's rights convention in Ohio in 1851, is the starting point for this chapter. Over 150 years later, Truth's words continue to provide valued currency for feminist discourses that at one and the same time seek to unify women and, crucially for Black women, to authorize the significance of difference. Donna Haraway (1992) suggests this is because in deconstructing the 'terrible edifice of "woman" in Western patriarchal language and systems of representation' (Haraway, 1992: 92), Sojourner Truth challenges the idea of the Black woman as one who can never be a subject, who is only 'plot space, matrix, ground, screen for the act of man'. Historically, this 'act of man' has been concerned with the racialized and sexualized objectification of the Black woman to service the interests of male desire and White privilege, while her exoticization has ensured the marginalization of her versions of womanhood.

The social construction and appropriation of the visual imagery of Black people to fuel racism and feed sexual appetites is of course as much a contemporary issue as it is a historical one. The case of Sarah Baartman, however, an enslaved South African woman, who during the early part of the nineteenth century was objectified in the most literal sense, vividly illustrates the point. (Sarah is sometimes referred to as Sara in the literature.) Taken to Europe, Sarah was presented in near-nakedness to exhibit her distinctly un-European anatomy, large breasts and bottom and her enlarged labia (a presumed attribute since she refused to show her genitals) (Willis, 2010). These features, embodied within a Black skin, gave her status as object a duality: given the historical, geographical and racially constructed space she occupied, it was assumed to be a 'fact' of nature that she should be a slave but it was as 'freak' of nature that her worth was measured. To be worked to death in the fields might not have been preferable, but the alienation, isolation and ridicule she must have endured while exhibited as some alien being would surely have crushed the soul. Sarah was gawped at, laughed at and prodded; although she was ultimately able to buy her freedom, servicing desire was all she knew and she died a destitute prostitute (Willis, 2010).

Death bestowed no reprieve from indignity: Sarah's body was dissected and bequeathed as a trophy to the Museum of Natural History in Paris. As recently as the 1970s, visitors to the Museum of Man could view her brain, skeleton and genitalia, although by then there was a groundswell of revulsion at her inhumane treatment and when Nelson Mandela became president of South Africa, he insisted that the French government release her remains. Born in 1789, and buried over 200 years later in 2002, Sarah was finally laid to rest in the land from which she had been taken (Willis, 2010).

If in life the exploitation of Sarah's body had taken a primarily sexualized form, in death it was distinctly racialized. The authorities had acceded to the museum's request to retain her corpse on the grounds that it represented an interesting specimen of humanity, her body a 'rhetorical artefact' in furtherance of the pseudoscientific determinism of the day, with its preoccupation with proving the biological inferiority of Black people (Gilchrist and Thompson, 2012). As Gilchrist and Thompson point out 'Representations, definitions, and treatments of the body are inherently political statements because of what they communicate about the constitutive meanings, importance, obsessions, practices, and urgencies related to the body' (Gilchrist and Thompson, 2012: 279). The racialized, sexualized and gendered politics of the flesh (body politics) that govern the meanings assigned to the relationship between biology and ideology are as much a feature of contemporary societies as they were of Baartman's time and perhaps even more so, given the universal reach of popular media (Spellers and Moffitt, 2010). Further, as Jackson (2006) contends, the interrogation of present-day Black body politics would be deficient without its historical context because some modern representations and imagery concerning the Black body can be regarded as 'contemporaneous with slavery' (Jackson, 2006: 12), feeding off the stereotypes imbued with emphasized sexuality, aggression, victimhood, dysfunction and intellectual inferiority that race constructions generate:

> Since the emergence of race as a social construct, Black bodies have become surfaces of racial meanings. So it is only logical that any attempt to divorce the concept of race from body politics leaves the analysis incomplete.
>
> (Jackson, 2006: 12)

The exhibitions featuring Sarah Baartman underscore the interplay between dominant conceptions of feminine beauty/ugliness and of racial inferiority. Along with the commoditization of Black women's sexuality (hooks, 1997), these dynamics feed what Haraway (1989) refers to as the imperialist fantasies associated with colonial domination that are encoded within such 'taxidermic displays'. As Cheng (2000) states:

> The works of Meg Armstrong, Emmanuel Eze, Henry Louis Gates, Sander L. Gilman, and Paul Gilroy, among others, have demonstrated the historic complicity between the philosophical discourse of aesthetic judgment and a meta-physics of racial difference since the Enlightenment. Aesthetic standards have often been deployed by thinkers from Immanuel Kant to Thomas Jefferson as literally the last moral ground on which to justify racist practices.
>
> (Cheng, 2000: 192)

Baartman was not by any Eurocentric measure considered beautiful at all, even though she had been described as a striking African beauty (Willis, 2010). However, as Lovejoy states:

> In the contested realm of Baartman's career, it was not a sense of 'beauty' that was the main attraction, but her divergence from European conceptions of the female body, which effectively made her a 'freak' suitable for public display, ridicule, and marvel.
>
> (Lovejoy, 2007: 3)

We pause here to acknowledge that feminist scholars have produced an extensive body of work concerning concepts of beauty, in their focus on the idealized and the imagined. These concepts are coercive and exploitative of women, and their ethnocentric biases construct aesthetic standards that are partial and exclusive (Cheng, 2000). The commoditization of beauty, with its relentless mission to make the unbeautiful beautiful, includes established standards that are marketed as pro-woman. In actuality, this 'discourse of ideality' promotes and services patriarchal interests, and an aversion to non-idealized femininities that is anti-woman since it undermines self-representation. Beauty is at the same time, then, a discourse of the 'unlovely' (Cheng, 2000), and both are used to feed sexual desires: while the idealized version of femininity may dominate the hegemonic porn culture, the woman who is deemed ugly, monstrous or different represents a different type of sexual conquest and adventure to satisfy the fetishes of those whose interests may be considered deviant or perverse.

This explains the fascination with Sarah Baartman who, though considered the antithesis of beauty, symbolized a 'wild, untamed sexuality' (Holmes, 2007). The obsession with Sarah's physical attributes was also a form of 'scientific pornography' (Holmes, 2007) because she was used not only to promulgate a 'primitive' Black sexuality for the titillation of White men, but also to further the science that established that the place of the Black African was as link between man and ape in the evolution of Homo sapiens (Lovejoy, 2007). The dehumanization that resulted in Sarah Baartman being reduced to her sexual parts was only made possible because of gendered and racist social constructions that positioned her as 'plot space'. Though at the centre of dominant Victorian discourse on the nature of the Black woman, Sarah Baartman was entirely peripheral to it; she may have been physically present in the stories that circulated about her but, as a female African slave, her own voice was perpetually absent (Holmes, 2007; Willis, 2010).

If it were ever possible to reduce the Abasindi Cooperative to an *essence*, this is the assertion we would make: that in the 200 years since Baartman's birth and the political, social and cultural activism in the wake of Sojourner Truth's historic speech, the Black woman has sought to position herself as subject rather than as backcloth to the tapestry of someone else's design. The Abasindi woman was plot – not plot space. And it is as plot that Abasindi asserted its own aesthetic standards of beauty. Sarah Baartman's story reminds us that the attribution of meanings of beauty may reflect differential experiences for Black women than for White women since, as Cheng observed, Sarah could not 'be made beautiful even in the imagination since her body is radically undisciplinable' (Cheng, 2000: 192).

The celebration of skin, body and hair that surfaced within the context of the Abasindi Cooperative suggested a conscious act of insurgency – a political activism of sorts. But conscious or not, the championing of hair left natural and the perfecting of African hair styles, the love of Black skin rather than its grading by shade and the assertion that the Black woman's body, however shaped, is unto itself beautiful, but more than this, is hers and hers alone, was undoubtedly an act of reclamation. Being part of Abasindi enabled the woman to reclaim for the self an aesthetic standard of choice and to celebrate, no, flaunt the joy of a female body that is undisciplinable:

> Maga women
> Strike poses in 6, 8, 10; sizes
> Of sharp angled hips
> Stomachs iron flat
> And breast-less silhouettes
> In clothed enviable perfection
>
> But nakedness reveals
> Knee bones protruding

> Thighs calves forearms twinning
> And arses hard to recognise.
>
> These are the models
> That sashay across our vision
> As we purse our lips
> In dismay disgust dejection
>
> While our hands caress
> The rise of belly
> That folds into an apron of warm flesh
>
> When we bend our breasts lead
> Identical dancers in motion
> The dimples of our elbows are deep
> Our knees are satin cushions
> Our lips cheek full
> And when we turn to leave
> Our hips are pivoting sensuality
>
> But we are not stereotype caricatures of Africa
> Maga women
> Come in shades
> Black and White
> As do we
> As do we.
>
> ('Maga Women', SuAndi © 2014)

That the beauty discourse has been used to control women's bodies was well understood within the organization but we did not accept that the idealization of particular notions of beauty that has been the source of much White feminist opposition should necessarily speak in the same way to Black women, since we are excluded for different reasons:

> Much of what has been written about beauty's relationship to femininity speaks sometimes with and sometimes without self-consciousness to and from an exclusively middle-class White paradigm. And much of what has been written about beauty's relationship to racism has presumed that a racialised individual's relationship to gender discriminations is analogous to, if it does not simply double, the burdens of racial oppression. But at the conjunction of racial and gender discriminations stands the woman of color, for whom 'beauty' presents a vexing problem

> both as judgment and solution. That is, between a feminist critique of feminine beauty and a denial of non-white beauty according to racial stereotyping, where does this leave the woman of color? Can she or can she not be beautiful? Is her beauty (or potential for beauty) good or evil? It is unclear whether assenting to the prospect of a 'beautiful woman of color' would be disruptive of racist discourse or complicit with gender stereotypes.
>
> (Cheng, 2000: 191)

Abasindi women, like Sojourner Truth and many women's activists since, believed that reclaiming representations of Blackness contained the potential to unsettle universalisms about dominant prescriptions of beauty that constrain all women – but also to confront racist ideologies within which these prescriptions are embedded and that constrain the freedom of Black women in particular. For the Black woman, then, it is not only the fields, the workplace, the family or the institutions that have been the site of her struggles but also her skin, her body and her hair. It is not that the organization abandoned the call to sisterhood generated by feminist opposition to the idealization of beauty, but this was not grounded in shared positionings that incorporated race, culture or historical legacy. The Abasindi women constructed an alternative discursive tradition based on reclamation, self-representation and the preservation of *their* versions of beauty. The theoretical anchor for this type of political activism is summed up thus:

> It is our task to make a place for this different social subject. In so doing we are less interested in joining the ranks of gendered femaleness than gaining the insurgent ground as female social subject.
>
> (Spillers cited in Li, 2006: 14)

And it was as female social subject that Sojourner Truth fought. Those familiar with her story will recall that a White male doctor protested the authenticity of her claim for equal rights and demanded that she prove she was a woman by showing her breasts. This was not simply an attempt to destroy agency by reducing the argument to anatomy, it was an exasperated outcry at the audacity that this physical manifestation of the Black unlovely should apply to the claim for rights that the White woman asserted. Truth owned rather than minimized her Blackness – the discourse she engendered was for a 'collective humanity' that challenged the reification of Whiteness and the whitening of Blackness to make the Black presence more acceptable.

She stepped out of her assigned role as plot space to centre herself as plot. Such a bold position was anathema to White patriarchal supremacists then and remains significant for contemporary times too. In recounting Truth's story, Haraway explains:

> Difference (understood as the divisive marks of authenticity) was reduced to anatomy; but even more to the point, the doctor's demand articulated the racist/sexist logic that made the very flesh of the black person in the New World indecipherable, doubtful, out of place, confounding –ungrammatical. Remember that Trinh Minh-ha, from a different Diaspora over a hundred years later, wrote, 'Perhaps, for those of us who have never known what life in a vernacular culture is/was and are unable to imagine what it can be/could have been, gender simply does not exist otherwise than grammatically in language.' Truth's speech was out of place, dubious doubly; she was female and black; no, that's wrong she was a black female, a black woman, not a coherent substance with two or more attributes, but an oxymoronic singularity who stood for an entire excluded and dangerously promising humanity. The language of Sojourner Truth's body was as electrifying as the language of her speech.
>
> (Haraway, 1992: 92)

Although a free woman, Truth's skin, body and hair, like Baartman's, were the symbols of a status deemed so inferior as to deny the right of the vote to someone not enough a human and not enough a woman to justify it. Yet Truth claimed these attributes as a voice with which to speak for Black women; the assertion 'ain't I a woman?', though essentially a rebuttal of the notion that Black women should not be allowed the suffrage rights White women were fighting for, also cut the heart out of the idea that femininity equals White. With the vote established some 60 years before the birth of the Abasindi Cooperative and held firmly under the belts of its members, the aesthetic claims about Black skin, body and hair functioned as a symbol of resistance to the continued post-suffrage oppressions that many Black women in Britain faced. Armed with our Afros, cornrows, braids and locks, we were ready to do battle on several fronts and we organized around issues such as the lack of educational opportunity for Black women and children, domestic violence, the impact of immigration controls, the marginalization of Black art and the criminalization of Black young people (discussed later in the book). Within a race-conscious society such as Britain, Black femininity cannot be taken for granted; however, the matter-of-factness of its existence among the Abasindi women and the loving of attributes associated with it – names, accents, art, body, skin and hair – established its prominence within the communities of Manchester in ways that were political, oppositional and affirmational. Trinh Minh-ha (1989) suggests that those of us who inhabit Diasporic spaces live outside of vernacular cultures, yet the accounts of Abasindi women suggest that they created a vernacular culture of their own. This is illustrated in the reflection below.

> **YINKA**
> My mother is one of the Abasindi women. This is a fact that I am proud of but don't often think about. The true impact of these women's history I haven't ever fully acknowledged ... I've somewhat taken it for granted, this legacy I've inherited and become slightly blasé about.
>
> The beginnings of these relationships were so organic and imbedded in my childhood that I am unaware of their inception. My mother had moved us back to London by the time I was 3 in order to be closer to our biological family, but many a school vacation was spent in Manchester. Abasindi morphed from its original home in a squat to various people's homes when the building threatened to collapse. I relished the opportunities I got to watch these women in action, and they always seemed to be in their element. As a girl I loved to just sit and listen to them reminisce and tell stories – these women are all my aunts and their children, my cousins. These occasions/moments were a major part of my development and socialization. I was provided with feminist opinions before I ever knew the terminology. Simply being in the company of Black women who were proud to be just that allowed me to love my Blackness in its totality, long before society at large had a chance to label me 'other' and cause me to question the validity and value in my beauty. I think of those times as the sowing of seeds on very fertile ground.
>
> There was no definitive moment or conversation where I was told that being Black was a thing to be proud of. I don't remember being told to love my hair, complexion, shape or any of the things I am instructed by society at large to be ashamed of. It just came with the territory I was in, the women of the proverbial village that my mother raised me in. These women came in various shades of Blackness and body shapes; these were my norms. In a world that tends to marginalize Black women, Black women *were* my norm. Amazing! By virtue of

the environment I grew up in I have been very fortunate to have been able to avoid one of the major relationship pitfalls in the lives of many Black women – the one with her hair. For some reading this that may not be a particularly significant statement. But for others of you who have struggled with your hair and the inextricable relationship it has with your identity, never having been bound by these psychological issues is really a very powerful thing. I am extremely thankful for this reprieve and can only hope and pray that more women experience this freedom and find genuine acceptance and love of natural hair.

In saying all this, I was never very fond of my name, Yinka. Not because it is African, though. It has to do with my being disappointed in my parents' lack of creativity in choosing one of the commonest Yoruba names for me and not even giving me a middle name to fall back on. Even in that choice I am reminded of what a bold statement was being made in selecting an African name while living in the Western world. It is so strange being in a new environment in which people are learning my name for the first time and how in awe of its 'uniqueness' they are. However, this is nothing new. All my Abasindi cousins are mothered by Caribbean women who each made the decision to give them beautiful-sounding names with even more melodious meanings. Our mothers are the women of Abasindi; what else would you expect? This is the nature of the women who comprised Abasindi the movement. It was not a movement in theory alone. These women were not donning African clothes for show and fashion. Their belief in and commitment to all things Abasindi, in addition to the African and Caribbean culture, ran deep. So much so that before people laughed *with* people's African accents and not *at* them, I was always secure in my dual heritage and there was never any separation between the two in my mind. Black is and always will be Black.

A note here about the use of the term 'Blackness', which for the purposes of this book functions as shorthand for the myriad dimensions of the experiences and identities of Black people ('Black' being synonymous with the American expression, 'people of color'). These identities cut across historicized and contemporary considerations not only of race, but of gender, sexuality, ethnicity, nationality, language, religion, mixed heritage, and the intersection of these experiences. As illustrated in Yinka's account, for second, third or fourth generation Black people living in Britain, identity

Yinka with her Parents, Leslie and Pauline, at her Naming Ceremony

may also take a different form from that of their parents and grandparents. Abasindi did not hold with prescriptions of Blackness and acknowledged that though identities are influenced by social context, Black people are not fixed within or defined by a 'static system of social locations' (Hill Collins, 1998). It is, however, beyond the remit of this chapter to discuss identity and intersectionality in more depth and we refer the reader to the many excellent texts (for example, Hill Collins, 1998).

Participating in a collective where the ethos was one of political consciousness-raising, and from which Abasindi women were able to derive positive affirmation of the Black and beautiful, is not for all women, but at least this was available through the many grassroots Black and minority ethnic organizations that sprang up in Britain in the post-colonial years. Black children, however, have often lacked access to the places and spaces for affirmation of racial identity and their dependent status means that how they feel about themselves is usually contingent upon or influenced by values transmitted from the adults around them. Yinka's induction into Abasindi as a young girl was neither accidental nor incidental.

The Abasindi Cooperative had a deliberate strategy to foster self-love and to raise esteem, aspiration and achievement among Black children. This guided many of our activities and was given effect through the organization's Saturday schools, summer schools and the teaching of arts and crafts.

We also involved children in drama, poetry and cultural activities and we contributed to children's political education; they were with us when we discussed strategies to protect women and children from deportation; they came with us, in our bellies, in their pushchairs or strung together holding hands when we protested against apartheid, the proliferation of nuclear arms and the Israeli occupation of Gaza. And as they joined in the welcoming parties held for political activists fighting for liberation in countries such as South Africa, Nicaragua and Palestine, or to celebrate a visiting Black artist, they looked on perplexed at the different accents, names and cultural traditions our friends brought with them.

The most significant role Abasindi played in the lives of Black children was in the nurturing of a healthy and positive sense of identity. The importance of this cannot be overstated. Consider Pecola Breedlove, the young girl in Toni Morrison's first novel, *The Bluest Eye*, whose lot was to be born poor, Black and female and who desired nothing more than to have blue eyes. Denuded of the affirming benefits of being immersed in an environment in which being Black is as unremarkable, normative and esteemed as being White and where the markers of beauty and acceptance are not colour-coded, Pecola was convinced of her own ugliness and lack of worth. In a manner not unconnected to the views about Blackness that affected Sarah Baartman over two centuries earlier, Morrison's novel portrays a set of values predicated on the aesthetic merits of Whiteness and the intrinsic negativity of Blackness that can cause harm, confusion and distress to children.

Arts and crafts at the Summer School

For most Black children growing up in the UK, the Black people in their lives, with all their strengths and failings – mothers, fathers, grandparents, brothers and sisters as well as wider kinships – provide a point of reference for the formation of their own positive identities. But Black children denuded of Black family life may experience a sense of alienation from cultural, linguistic and religious heritage or they may try to construct an idealized identity based on either fictional or pathologized Black role models. One group of Black children who are particularly vulnerable in this regard are those who are brought up in local authority care. In the absence of alternative representations, these children often internalize the derogatory messages about Blackness that are pervasive in the values and attitudes of those around them, leading to feelings of rejection, self-deprecation and distorted perceptions of self-image (Ung *et al.*, 2012).

Clearly it is difficult to isolate the internalization of negative beliefs about the self as a cause of children's emotional and psychological problems because children in care have usually experienced a range of traumas, losses and disruptions that also generate these problems, but for some children this is a contributing factor. In his observations of the Black child in the British care system, Small argued over three decades ago that a healthy personality requires that the psychic image the child has of herself must match her reality (Small, 1984). However, if the child is not to be 'engulfed and rendered impotent by such negative social images' to which Black children are often exposed, he or she must also be able to 'transcend reality' (Barn, 2000: 7).

The fantasy of imagining herself with blue eyes was not evidence of Pecola's ability to escape her reality but the opposite: unable to transcend the reality of living in a world in which only little White girls could be beautiful she internalized negative representations of Blackness. Her search for blue eyes was in actuality a search for confirmatory signs of her own unloveliness, and though the harm was initially felt only inside her, in time realization of the immutability of being Black led to a destructive rage that she began to externalize. Yet Pecola grew up in the midst of her family; she was not taken into care, she did not grow up in a children's home, or a transracial foster or adoptive home.

Immersion within a Black family may not of itself provide Black children with the emotional scaffolding to be able to transcend the reality of living in a racist environment if adults have themselves internalized negative portrayals of Black people and transmit these to their offspring. The creation of a healthy and positive identity over the lifespan is not about achieving congruence between perceptions of self and constructions of race (or of gender, sexual orientation or any other aspects of identity) because in environments in which destructive messages are prevalent, it is a transcendental imagination that is needed, the capacity, such as that possessed by Sojourner Truth, to fashion oneself from a position of equal human value outside of the myopic lens of racism. Like many Black children in care, 'Pecola interprets poor treatment and abuse as her own fault. She believes that the way people observe her is more reliable than what she herself observes' (Morrison, 1999: 38); because her eyes are not blue she is inferior, unworthy and unlovable. Abasindi women came across many Black children in the care system who were in search of blue eyes and who seemed to have few opportunities for the loving of Blackness. Below, one of the women who adopted a Black child after a series of failed White foster placements reflects on her son's silent transformation to becoming Black:

My son came to me when he was six; he had last had contact with his father, who had been the only Black person in his life, when he was just a baby and had never been close to another Black man since. His distorted views of himself spilled out onto his drawings; he was the little White boy with yellow hair living in a little house with a White mum and dad. At first he gravitated to any and all Black men we met; it seemed to me as if he wanted to drink up their Blackness. But this meant he was vulnerable, he would have gone off with anyone. I took him with me to Abasindi, to all the meetings we had, the music and dance sessions, the Saturday school and through the Black women he met there, he was introduced to their fathers, husbands, brothers, uncles, friends, and learned almost by osmosis who to trust and who to steer away from. Black people had been extraordinary to him and it was only when they became part of his everyday ordinariness that he could take his little Black self for granted. His early lessons about the beautiful kind of Black man he could, and would, become were learned at the feet of Black women.

(Abasindi woman – anonymous)

As in other indicators of social inequality, Black children have long been disproportionately represented within the UK care system (Owen and Statham, 2009). This can be partly explained by the fact that among the myriad factors that may lead to a child being received into care are those that particularly affect Black families, such as poverty, social and economic disadvantage, poor housing, unemployment and parental ill health (Pilkington, 2003). Children are also taken into care because they are the victims of abuse or neglect, because they have become separated from their families, as in the case of young asylum seekers, or because parents

Abasindi boys

are unable to care for them. Barn and Kirton reported that there were 67,050 children in local authority care in England in 2012, of whom 16 per cent were Black children of African or African-Caribbean descent (Barn and Kirton, 2012), yet only around 3 per cent of the child population in the UK is from Black or Black British and Mixed groups (Harker and Heath, 2012).

For more than half a century local authorities have sought to resolve the problem of the disproportionate number of Black children in care by placing them in transracial placements. Transracial adoption and fostering refers to the placement of children across racial, religious and ethnic (and often geographic) boundaries and primarily involves White adults adopting non-White children. The practice is contentious, being ferociously defended by its proponents and severely criticized by those who consider this to be but another example of the domination and exploitation of one group by another (Ung *et al.*, 2012). The Black or minority ethnic child adopted into a family that lacks a reference point to their racial or cultural heritage is subjected to compounded forms of disadvantage. Ung *et al.* state:

> If this familial situation extends to the community and social holding environment of the adopted person, such that their genetic and visual racial group is not mirrored for them in their social environment, there is, according to the prevailing body of literature, little opportunity for her or him to acquire and achieve positive self-regard in relation to self and race, or reconciliation of racial conflict.
>
> (Ung *et al.*, 2012: 76)

This issue seems to be little understood by those who hold the power to determine policy on Black children in care; from where they sit, to be in search of blue eyes may seem a small price to pay for life in a foster or adoptive family. The minimizing of the importance of racial, cultural, linguistic and familial heritage for Black children, however, reflects some fundamental inequalities within the care system and, as Barn (2000) points out in relation to transracial placements, White children 'have not had to experience a similar [racial/cultural] upheaval at a time of separation and loss from the birth family' (Barn, 2000: 9). This determinedly colour-blind policy agenda has been employed by successive UK governments and masks an integrationist approach that fails to address the structural inequalities that affect Black children and families. Implicit in adoption discourses are deeply embedded notions of racial superiority and inferiority that position White, heteronormative and middle class as best (Barn, 2000: 13). That these strategies should be implemented within the context of an intently race-conscious society, in which the agenda of all political shades – from liberal to far-right – is preoccupied with the 'foreign invasion', and the increasing control and surveillance of Black people, is an irony that cuts deep. From the perspective of Black people, young people brought up in the care system have often reported a 'sense of isolation and alienation, of being "dropped in a white sea", and of discrimination, lack of understanding or culturally insensitive provision [that] sadly remain a reality for some young Black and minority ethnic children in residential child care' (Voice for the Child in Care, 2004: 1).

In Abasindi there were women who had grown up in care themselves and who had sought out the group to help counter the effects of living one's childhood in a world impacted by racist constructions and at the same time devoid of positive racial, cultural or linguistic anchor points. Other Abasindi women came into contact with Black children in care through their work as social workers and psychologists and some were the foster parents and adoptive mothers who looked after them. In the 'Letter to a social worker' below, one of these women seeks to unmask the collusion of professionals in a system established on the assumptions of White as normative and Black as problematic in decisions about the placement of children. The letter is written in the style of Audre Lorde's 'An open letter to Mary Daly' (Lorde, 1979 in Lorde, 1984: 66–71).

> Dear Social Worker
>
> Identity is a complex, ever-changing and multidimensional concept in which we are always becoming who we are. The most significant experiences in shaping who I am now are those to do with being a mother, although these are indivisible from my own experiences of having been mothered and indeed, my experiences of being a sister, a friend, a partner, a worker or the many other roles that give my life meaning. I came to mothering through adoption and it is as a Black adoptive mother that I write. I do not write for all Black mothers although I believe that what I have to say will resonate with many of them, and also with Black fathers too. ... Your decisions about race and who should and should not adopt Black children are set within the agenda of the government of the day. That you might, of course, consider questions of race in the placement of a White child is something you keep quiet about. Far from this being an irrelevant factor in the placement of White children, the silence in which you take refuge simply masks the fact that such is the depth and extent of

consensus in assuming 'White' as normative that it does not even need to be stated. The assured, taken-for-granted status of 'Whiteness' and its associated meanings informs adoptive assessment, approval and matching processes so pervasively and completely it is their lifeblood; what then, can there possibly be to question?

This is a reminder to me that positions that benefit the dominant in society, unlike those of us struggling for recognition in the margins, rarely need to be defended and would never be subject to the charges of ideological radicalism those of us proclaiming the value of Black families have often faced. It also pointedly serves to underscore, should I be in any doubt, that my value to British society as a Black mother and my contribution to the lives of Black children is considered negligible at worst and minimal at best.

Instead of simply accepting transracial placements as a solution to the placement needs of Black children, perhaps you should question why so much political energy is invested in supporting this position? Why is it that opposition is couched as extremism – what deeply held perceptions of me as a Black woman could possibly demand or expect my acquiescence? Perhaps you should think about the ways in which public research into the private lives of Black transracially placed children subverts the ways in which children are impacted by the internalization of racism and the distortion of self-image. Why it is that there are no similar public studies of the strengths of Black family life and the ways in which these can provide the protective, nourishing and empowering factors to achieve the outcomes you have subscribed to for children? ...Why is it that you want to play down difference when discussing these issues yet you are among those who have benefited from the negative representations of difference in wider society just as surely as Black children have not? Why is it that there are so many Black children in local authority care and what is it that the liberal among you are *really* saying when you assert that it is in support of Black children that so many are placed transracially? Can you conceive of the possibility that from where I am sitting, liberalism, despite benevolent intentions, may not look benign at all but may mask or perpetuate inequalities? And why must the lid be kept on racism, for this is what lies at the root of this discussion? I would like to see it raised up, so I can stamp on its head. And you, can it be that you are prepared to settle for avoiding discomfort rather

> than fighting for human rights and social equality that might attend to the needs of Black children and families?
>
> My comments are not about racial purity. I am not an advocate of clumsy experiments in colour or ethnicity matching and I am not the hostile voice of anti-White rebellion. It is simply that being denuded of the experience of growing and living among Black people is an impoverishing experience for Black children and for the Black people who have so much to give and to gain by becoming their parents. It adds the loss of racial and cultural context to the losses a child in care may already be dealing with (I make this point in the belief that people must not be reduced to definitive, static or homogenizing notions of race and culture and I also acknowledge that for many Black people, culture includes perceptions and experiences of Britishness and so on). It reduces Black children's opportunities for positive affirmation of themselves as Black people and for many Black children (this is the case regardless of the 'success' stories you would remind me of) is often the source of distress and searching in later years.
>
> Perhaps when you have considered all of these questions, you will think about how you burden Black children with these weighty matters and also reflect on the messages you give to Black adults, for this may help to explain why it is that they may not be willing to come forward to offer themselves as parents to the children in your care.
>
> Anonymous (adapted from 'Letter to a social worker: Reflections on mothering', in Douglas and Philpot, 2003, 91–8)

The manifestations of internalized racism include loathing of the physical characteristics associated with being Black such as skin colour and hair texture, stereotyping, denial of heritage, beliefs about White superiority and Black inferiority, and over-identification with people who derogate Black people. Black children may be subject to racial taunts, bullying, direct acts of discrimination and pervasive negative messages about Black people, or they may witness White children receiving preferential treatment. Cemented by structural inequalities and institutional racism, Black young people may come to view the lack of opportunity and the challenges in achieving aspirations as being attributable to their physical characteristics rather than to the social constructions spun around racial (and gendered) differences on which systems of domination and exclusion have been built:

> It is now commonly recognized that black children face much greater difficulty in handling racism and clarifying their own sense of self if they are brought up in settings and neighbourhoods lacking positive role models.
>
> (Chakrabarti and Hill, 2000: 23)

Adults who are able to empathize with these experiences and provide explanations about the history and nature of racism can counteract the destructive force of these dynamics and prevent their translation into beliefs about low self-worth. Research by The Voice for the Child in Care found that Black families may be the main, or even only, 'gateway' through which Black children in care can access their cultural and ethnic identity, whereas White children growing up in a predominantly White society have countless role models to draw upon. Where these protective factors are absent from the child's environment, however, the internalization of racism may result in harmful behaviours being directed at the self or being externalized through antisocial acts, aggression or bullying. These manifestations are the surface expressions of negative beliefs about the self that often reflect deeper psychological problems with implications for mental well-being and interpersonal relationships across the lifespan.

The extent and depth of the difficulties internalized racism can cause can never be known, but the physical neglect of the loving of Blackness was often evident in the children in care that we came across. Theirs was the hair left uncombed, un-oiled or cut short because it was simply too much trouble, and theirs was the Black skin left uncared for from lack of moisturizing cream so that, in the cold of Britain, they turned grey, ashen, dry and mottled. These were the children who settled for being unlovely – because, like Pecola, they observed themselves through a prism of racial deprecation; a very subtle process that is all the more powerful for that fact. They were the Black boys first to be excluded from school and sent to pupil referral units for behavioural problems (Gillborn, 2004; Graham and Robinson, 2004) and they were the girls most likely to be sexually exploited by the older men who use gendered power and status to feed on their vulnerabilities (Jones and Jemmott, 2014).

Of course, there are many Black children in care who do well, who thrive regardless of, or perhaps because of, the care they have received and whose own family life would have been dismal but for intervention by the state. There are foster and adoptive parents, Black and White, who have loved Black children beyond measure; indeed the colour of skin is no indicator of the capacity for parental love, as the countless number of Black children with 'mixed' (one Black and one White) parents can testify. But for the Black child removed from his/her birth family and then submerged in a world where colour, name, hair, religion, accent or nationality were the source of humour, derision or discrimination, Abasindi provided an opportunity to feel good about him/herself. It was unsurprising therefore that among all the children brought to Abasindi to have their hair braided or styled in cornrows, several lived in children's homes or foster homes; the decision to positively embrace their hair was an act of self-affirmation and resilience.

MELANIE

Visualize proud, beautiful Black women. Women of all ages, beautiful shades of the blue/black/brown hue, and shapes and sizes. Each woman resplendent, every one different, each has their own individual style. They ranged from beautiful to attractive and everything in between, with an eclectic mix of lengths in hairstyles and shapes. There were sisters wearing locks, plaits, threading and cornrow. As I lovingly take care of my own natural hair, I give thanks and gratitude to the women who taught me to appreciate it.

Hair was one of the things Abasindi was famous for. As any number of women sat around a huge table, talking, debating and arguing while being beautified, I would spend hours blending into the group as I waited my turn to take my seat in the chair, to have my hair cornrowed; I wondered what I would be transformed into, but I was never disappointed. The talking never stopped and there would be several conversations going on at once. They made cornrows fashionable at a time when identity was an issue.

Braiding hair at Abasindi

Hyacinth's hairstyle is a combination of cornrow and braids

Historically, Black people's hair has been a visible stigma of Blackness second only to skin (Mercer, 1999). For African people in the Diaspora, the emergence of the Afro in the 1960s represented a rejection of 'good' hair and its association with Whiteness, acceptance and social status, and a celebration of hair that is naturally kinky and curly. Braiding, dreadlocks and the Afro emerged as politicized statements of pride and empowerment (hooks, 1997; Weekes, 1997).

However, as bell hooks argued, 'even during the most militant stages of Black power movement, [women] had never really stopped allowing racist notions of beauty to define female desirability' (hooks, 1994: 177) and for many the natural look was simply a transient fad. Nyamnjoh *et al.* (2002) go further in their exploration of the modernization of African hairstyles in Cameroon. They suggest that it was not so much politicization but the romanticization of an 'Africanist heritage' during the 1960s, 1970s and 1980s that resulted in the popularization of the Afro, cornrows and beaded plaits (Nyamnjoh *et al.*, 2002: 107) and this, they argue, explains its ephemeral status. Nevertheless hair, however fashioned, has remained one of the defining characteristics of Blackness.

For the last three decades at least, a global market of straighteners, weaves and wigs has fuelled consumption patterns that replicate Western aesthetic values. Nyamnjoh *et al.* (2002) suggest this is not an abandonment of the traditional but the constant re-invention of self through aesthetic choices that reflect a distancing from the past and an engagement with the modern. They argue that Black women use these products from economic and creative choice and that the styles they create, though influenced by socialization processes underpinned by hegemonic versions of beauty, do not emulate Western styles but are distinctive to Black women. Although the study by Nyamnjoh and colleagues is of African women in Cameroon, the insights generated are more widely applicable and demonstrate that between the forces of globalization and the aesthetic values generated from localized contexts, the use of 'shampoos and conditioners, straighteners and dyes, curlers and blowdriers create new spaces in which women make themselves neither according to conservative local structures nor in the exact image of the west' (Nyamnjoh *et al.*, 2002: 102). These Black women are not necessarily less politically astute than those who choose natural or traditional African hairstyles but 'consumers living within the modernist aesthetic [who] constantly attempt to negotiate the rupture between creativity and (imaginative but co-opting) consumption' (Nyamnjoh *et al.*, 2002: 101). Meaning-making in relation to the adoption of false or straightened hair is therefore owned as much by the women who wear these styles as it is by those who dominate the reproduction of representations of beauty. These women may not be centre plot in the subject–object dynamic of representational body politics, but neither are they plot space – they are neither mime nor counterfeit. Mercer explains:

> When hairstyling is critically evaluated as an aesthetic practice inscribed in everyday life, all black hairstyles are political in that they each articulate responses to the panoply of historical forces which have invested this element of the ethnic signifier with both symbolic meaning and significance.
>
> (Mercer, 1994: 104)

A woman who relaxes her hair, wears a wig or a weave does not do so in a political or cultural vacuum; indeed her agential choices, inimitably connected as these are to the underlying morass of a racialized aesthetic, may reflect a knowing subjectivity that traverses between the creative, the pragmatic and the self-representational. Modern-day feminist theory must be able to embrace the idea that alongside the reclamation of Black natural hair, the bewigged versions of the Black aesthetic also contain possibilities for 'postcolonial, nongeneric, and irredeemably specific figures of critical subjectivity, consciousness, and humanity – not in the sacred image of the same, but in the self-critical practice of difference' (Haraway, 1992: 87).

Hairstyles are associated with professional standing, occupation and prestige, and are imbued with meaning about conformity, morality, wealth and social status. Thompson (2009) suggests that Black women may choose to wear false or chemically straightened hair because they are acutely aware of the potentially negative impact 'an authentically Black aesthetic will create' (Thompson, 2009: 852). Thompson offers one explanation for the choices Black women make but she makes a larger point too – the discursive realm of Black hair is not simply a binary of polarized opposites between the 'natural', constituted as expression of political agency, and the 'unnatural', viewed as a surrender of sorts, but represents the entanglement of race, politics and history with popular culture and the subjective constructions of Black beauty within specific lived realities (Brown, 2014).

Drawing on the work of Hill Collins, Brown (2014) argues that Black women have responded to hegemonic prescriptions of beauty by adopting a dual consciousness that enables them both to embrace, and even adopt, the aesthetics arising out of relations of oppression publicly, while in their private spaces and subjective standpoints they remain acutely oppositional to racist constructions (Brown, 2014: 10). As Marco states, 'positioning the Black self in this political culture is constant' (Marco, 2012: 30).

What this discussion highlights is that given the social conditioning of dominant representations of beauty, the internalization of racism that can lead to despising Black hair, the pathologizing of some natural styles and a socio-economic climate in which natural hairstyles may limit Black women's career and relationship prospects, the choice of the Afro, cornrow, plaits or dreadlocks represents both a personal choice and a political standpoint. And it is not only in relation to Black women that this matters; it matters to children too. In a UK landmark case, the High Court determined that a school's refusal to allow a Black boy to wear his hair in cornrow plaits was racial discrimination. The school had banned an 11-year-old African-Caribbean pupil because his hairstyle was said to breach the school's dress code and could be viewed as gang-related. Although the headteacher made it clear that he did not directly associate cornrow plaits with gang violence, he believed 'that allowing the wearing of any non-traditional haircut would lead to "huge pressure" to unravel a strict policy which was "a vital part" of the school's success in keeping out unwanted influences' (Loveys, 2011). The question arises, how does a Black boy fashion himself in a society in which a traditional African hairstyle leads to his exclusion from education because he is an 'unwanted influence'. Although the judge ruled the school's action to be 'unlawful, indirect racial discrimination which is not justified' (Loveys, 2011), the rallying cry in the school's defence was to draw attention to their excellent results and reputation, *even* among African-Caribbean families. It was as if the acquiescence of Black children and parents with racism was the price to be exacted for a decent education.

The Abasindi Cooperative offered a hairstyling service to women and children as a source of income, but also in support of those who sought to challenge the pervasive imposition of White ethnocentric values that this case highlights. For some Black children, the statement they make in choosing braids, cornrows or dreadlocks may indeed be reflective of the popular icons that have influenced them, but for others the statement is overtly political in its challenge to systems of domination. Like Black women, young people are bombarded by hegemonic images that seek to promulgate particular styles and they are the target for aggressive global marketing strategies for the consumption of products designed to promote universal representations of the popular and acceptable. But young people are masters in the art of weeding out norms masquerading as difference and whether they choose to weave or to 'Fro, these expressions of selfhood and imagination serve to 'deconstruct victimhood by reconstructing modernity, thus empowering those who would otherwise be disempowered in the end, both locally and by the giant compressors of global consumer capitalism' (Nyamnjoh *et al.*, 2002: 102). As Nyamnjoh *et al.* argue, both women and youth are particularly positioned to exercise this imaginative capacity, which both 'liberates and captures' (Nyamnjoh *et al.*, 2002: 102).

Since the Abasindi Cooperative was first established, there have been many shifts in Black hairstyles and there is a resurgent interest in natural hair (Brown, 2014). Brown (2014) utilized the social media site YouTube to examine the commentaries of Black women on natural hair styles. Established in 2005, YouTube is one of the world's most widely used websites, and has been described as helping to create community and preserve culture, and Brown's study identified that the values transmitted within this virtual community embodied sensibilities of both the Black feminism of earlier periods and also the post-feminist feminisms of the present. She concluded that:

Pauline

> Natural hair means *freedom*. For the women in YouTube's natural hair community naturally textured tresses mean liberation from the disparaging beliefs about Black hair that have been embedded in many of these women's psyches from birth by their family, communities and the aesthetic standards encouraged inside and outside of African American culture.
>
> (Brown, 2014: 78)

From the Abasindi standpoint, loving the Black body, loving Black skin and loving Black hair was indeed an expression of felt personal freedom;

Black beauty – Francia Messado

but as a collective, in reconfiguring beauty in the image of the Black women we were, the adornment and fashioning of our bodies, skin and hair was the articulation of an urgent political insurgency. Our approach to Black beauty was not simply a response to the psychic threat of the internalization of the racial disparagement used to justify Sarah Baartman's treatment and neither was it only emblematic of Sojourner Truth's act of non-compliance with structural locations that confine Black women: it was both. As Cheng (2000) points out, 'beauty as a process of identification registers her [the Black woman's] relationship to the education of beauty and to her history of negotiating that education – a negotiation of distances rather than an act only of internalization or compliance. Beauty as a question, as much as it may exclude her, also grants her an access to the intensities of its demands and its possibilities' (Cheng, 2000: 209).

Chapter 6
Sowing seeds of success

Introduction
While acknowledging that self-help voluntary projects could not by themselves change the political and economic conditions of Black people, Abasindi Cooperative nevertheless recognized the need for Black women to organize projects aimed at identifying and responding to their particular needs. As well as providing a social-supportive base for Black women and a community resource centre, Abasindi was also committed to the provision of supplementary and cultural educational activities for children and young people of African-Caribbean descent. The establishment of Abasindi Saturday supplementary school was based on the disproportionate levels of educational underachievement of Black children. The findings of Javed's 2012 research on the educational experiences of Black boys aged 13 to 16 in Manchester is further evidence of the need for Saturday supplementary schools. The involvement of Abasindi members in the development of the Louise Da-Cocodia Education Trust supplementary education programmes is an example of this. This chapter begins by looking chronologically at the racial and cultural issues that led to the establishment of Black supplementary schools. The role of Abasindi in the development of its Saturday Supplementary school during the 1980s is discussed, showing how this has in turn influenced current initiatives in the field of supplementary education.

Black supplementary schools
Chevannes and Reeves (1987) argue that the emergence of Black Saturday supplementary schools in the UK represents a collective response to the inadequate education available to Black children. The development of these schools was also directly linked to the experiences of migrant children during the period of assimilation. In 1965 the Department of Education and Skills (DES) defined the task of education as 'the successful assimilation of immigrant children'. This period of assimilation was further characterized by a series of ad hoc responses to the educational needs of immigrant pupils. These included strategies designed to compensate for their assumed deficiencies while causing minimum disruption to the educational needs of indigenous children. All this was taking place at a time when overtly

racist attitudes towards Black people were commonplace. In some areas advertisements for accommodation stated 'no coloured, no Irish, no dogs' (Webster, 1998: xiii). The 1963 Conference on Communication concluded that Creole languages were a major area of deficiency. As speakers of 'subnormal English', Black immigrant parents and their children were regarded as 'educationally subnormal' and as among those destined to occupy marginalized positions within British society (Dalphinis, 1978: 89).

The Plowden Report of 1967 was the first to draw attention to the poor performance of Black children when compared to their White working-class counterparts. On the recommendation of the 1973 Select Committee on Race and Immigration, the Rampton Committee was established, partly in response to the growing discontent among Black parents about the plight of their children in schools. The 1971 publication of Bernard Coard's book *How the West Indian Child is Made Educationally Sub-normal in the British Educational System* confirmed and highlighted the disproportionate number of African-Caribbean pupils in Educationally Sub-Normal (ESN) schools or special units for disruptive pupils.

At the 1995 Manchester Conference on 'Black Values versus State Education' organized by Beresford Edwards (Nana Bonsu), political activist and Warden of the West Indian Centre Carmoor Road, keynote speaker Trevor Carter, who served on the Rampton Committee Inquiry, stressed that the committee was unique in that for the first time the state, through the Department of Education and Science (DES), had acknowledged the existence of institutional racism. Carter argued that this acknowledgement was not a result of the actions of the handful of Black members on the committee, nor was it based on evidence gathered from schools and communities across the country. According to Carter, it was largely due to the 1981 nation-wide disturbances by unemployed and disaffected young Black people. The 1981 disturbances in Moss Side and South London are said to have 'shattered the mirage of assimilation and ushered in multiculturalism' (Sallah and Howson, 2007: 30).

Rampton stood down from the Committee of Inquiry, and in 1985, as the Swann Committee, the report *Education For All* was published by the DES. The Swann Report summed up the period of assimilation as 'one which gave recognition to the existence of a single cultural criterion, that which was 'White', 'Christian' and 'English speaking'. The language used reflected the values of this cultural criterion. It is therefore argued that schools serve as a vehicle through which the cultural capital and languages of subordinate classes are devalued (Bourdieu and Passerson, 1977).

Maureen Stone (1981) writes of the pain of being 'Black in England' and the shock and disappointment of parents who expected that their children, born and brought up in the UK, would not have to face the problems of settling in a new country and would have greater opportunity to succeed. The fear of further disadvantaging their children's educational prospects led to some ethnic minority parents insisting that their British-born children should only speak English at home. The concerns of parents were not unfounded. Some Manchester children, although British by birth, spent much of their formative years in the Caribbean. On returning to England, they often found themselves in classes that did not reflect their ability but rather reflected the perception of teachers that they could not speak English properly.

> I am one of the 50s children born in this country who was sent to Jamaica before I was a year old to be looked after by my grandparent. I was educated in Jamaica up to the age of 13 and then came back to England to join the secondary school system. I remember distinctively having to take a test which was all about the British experience. It was tailored towards their lifestyle and not a wider culture ... When we first started at the school, I felt a sense of strong injustice because both my sister and I were put into a lower class because of our dialect and not our academic ability.
>
> (Watt, 2002: 190)

In his discussions on Caribbean languages, Morgan Dalphinis (1978) argues that although the languages of West and sub-Saharan Africa were taken to the Caribbean, the system of separating speakers of the same languages ensured the suppression of the various mother tongues. This strategy was aimed at inhibiting rebellion among the enslaved. They were punished for speaking their own African languages by whipping and sometimes death. During the 1950s, students in Kenya were punished for speaking in their mother tongue and made to wear a 'monitor' with an inscription aimed at shaming the wearer: 'I am stupid I was caught speaking my mother tongue'. Students in Kenya are still threatened with the monitor and Wangari Maathai argues that its use

> ... contributes to the trivialization of anything African and lays the foundation for a deeper sense of self-doubt and an inferiority complex. The reality is that mother tongues are extremely important as vehicles of communication and carriers of culture, knowledge, wisdom and history. When they are maligned and

educated people are encouraged to look down on them, people are robbed of a vital part of their heritage.

(Maathai, 2007: 59–60)

Although each of the Caribbean languages was developed out of the language of the colonizers, they nevertheless maintained characteristics of speech that are directly associated with Africa (Dove, 1998). Louise Bennett (1966) was the first Jamaican poet formally to use Patois in her performances, and her poem 'Bans O'Killing' challenges perceived notions of language inferiority. The late Victoria McKenzie was among performing artists in Manchester who openly challenged the marginalization and denigration of Caribbean languages.

> **TRIBUTE TO VICTORIA MCKENZIE – JACKIE ROY**
> I'd asked a friend if she knew anyone who would be willing to teach me something about Jamaican Patois. It was the language my father had spoken, but he'd died when I was 7 and to this day, whenever I hear it spoken round me, I'm reminded of him, so it was important to me to become more familiar with it. I teach Caribbean literature and I also wanted to be able to recognize words and structures of the language. The friend I asked was also a member of Abasindi Cooperative and she told me that Victoria McKenzie, an active supporter of Abasindi was the person I should talk to. At the time, Vicky was in her 80s and had endured a lot of physical illness. She had suffered a great personal tragedy that had also taken its toll on her health. But as soon as I saw her, even though I met her on a day when she was unwell, I was struck by her inner vitality. This was a woman who could sparkle with enthusiasm and warmth. She welcomed me, a stranger, into her home and right from the start, she treated me as a friend.
>
> As I got to know her I realized that Victoria McKenzie was one of the most prominent members of the Caribbean community here in Manchester. She was a writer, producing performance poetry, and a community worker. She seemed to know everyone of Caribbean heritage in Manchester and had plenty of stories to tell. She had come to Britain while relatively young and had raised family here. She told me that it had been impossible in those early years for a Black woman to gain access to higher education or to find success as any kind of artist. She spoke of the obstacles she'd come up against, the racism she'd experienced, and the differences between generations.

Her generation had mostly been unable to fulfil their potential but she and others had made damn sure that subsequent generations would have the opportunities that had been denied to her. She spoke with pride about the achievements of younger Black writers, friends like Lemn Sissay and Pete Kalu, and never once displayed any kind of envy. All her energy went into supporting others, and although she did find success as a poet later in life, she never allowed that success or ambition to make her competitive or self-serving. She was someone who gave everything she could to further the education and the creative activities of the Caribbean community as a whole.

One of Vicky's great successes was producing a book in Patois. She'd become aware that children who spoke Patois were disadvantaged in British schools and she worked to dispel the misapprehension that Patois characterized its speakers as unintelligent or uneducated. One of her main missions was to get Patois recognized as a language in its own right – it's not an inferior form of English or simply the language of the streets, it's a language that empowers its speakers and gives them the right to their own cultural, social and political identity. Vicky promoted Patois as all these things and went into schools and community projects to remind everyone of its value.

In one of the calendars on Celebrating Black History in Trafford there is a wonderful photo of Vicky, her face alight with laughter, looking as if she's about to give a reading. Beneath this is her personal statement and, for me, this sums up the kind of person she was. She said: 'We can achieve anything we want from the seeds our parents did plant'.

Abasindi Saturday Supplementary School

Within the Black community, success is often linked to educational achievements. Parental influence, community projects and cultural activities were cited as contributing to the academic success of African-Caribbean people in the UK (Rhamie and Hallam, 2002). hooks (2003) sees education as taking place not only in the classroom but wherever people are and, as elsewhere in the country, Coard's work was central to the development of Abasindi Saturday Supplementary School in Moss Side. A large percentage of supplementary school programmes were organized by women. Hey (1998: 20) differentiates between male strategies for securing social resources, and female strategies for constructing social capital in order to develop effective community links as 'his and hers' approaches to community. Abasindi Saturday School was built on 'her' version in the sense that it was mainly women that were responsible for its organization and the recruitment of Black university students, male and female, as voluntary tutors.

Roy Blackman and Elouise Edwards

In addition to providing supplementary lessons, especially in mathematics and English, the programme focused on what Coard described as 'tools to survive racism'. This concerns Black children's sense of identity, pride and belonging (Andrews, 2013: 6). Clark and Clark's (1939, 1947) classic doll studies demonstrated that 35 per cent of 6 year olds identified with the Black doll but 60 per cent expressed preference for White dolls and 59 per cent said that the Black doll 'looked bad'. Similar results were obtained in England, and in his study of 7, 8, 9 and 10 year olds, Davey (1983) found that 86 per cent of White children regarded their own group more favourably than either African-Caribbean or Asian children. Less than half of the African-Caribbean and Asian children made 'own group choice'. Davey concluded that both minority and majority children saw the advantage of being White. Maxime (1986) described the case of a 12-year-old Black boy who from the age of 6 had lived with White foster parents in a middle-class area on the outskirts of London. A racial identity assessment revealed that he viewed Black people negatively and saw himself as someone who was trapped in the colour of his skin.

One of the best-known models of Black identity development is Cross's (1971) five-stage model of 'Nigresence', the psychological process individuals go through in their journey towards a secure and confident Black identity. Cross argues that in the initial pre-encounter a person's world view is White-oriented and they are likely to deny the existence of racism. The encounter stage is linked to experiences or observations that bring the person face-to-face with racism and the realities of being Black. The immersion-emersion stage involves critical exploration of issues of race and culture, and the internalization stage represents a conscious move towards the development of a positive Black identity. The final stage of the model is internalization-commitment. Maxime (1986) found that students with high levels of Black identification were more likely to participate in activities involving the Black community.

Abasindi women at the Supplementary School (Diana and Paula)

At the 2005 Black Perspective in Community and Youth Work Conference in Manchester, Blackburn (2005) drew on the findings of her 2001 study to highlight the limitations of Cross's psychological Nigresence model. She argued that the DAISE model, a synthesis of Cross (1971), Parham (1989) and Phinney (1990), was much more relevant to understanding the stages of Black identity undergone by a broader range of people. In the dormant stage of this cyclical model Black identity is not fully developed and there is a general tendency for the person to lack interest in and knowledge about their cultural heritage. However, during the awakening stage of identity development, and consistent with the African proverb 'It takes a village to raise a child', Abasindi ensured that the organization provided a culturally supportive environment for the children and young people attending the Saturday school.

> It was just like a huge family – everybody knew each other's kids, and if my mum wasn't around somebody was always there for me ... Those are some of the things that I miss for my daughter because my mum lived in London, raising her has been lonely especially when I look back to those times in Abasindi when there were lots of aunties and uncles to nurture and make you feel safe. That is why as a Black woman I have always been proud of myself.
>
> (Anonymous – Abasindi member)

The awakening stage is similar to Cross's (1971) encounter stage in relating to experiences of racism and sense of self. Most of the children who attended the Saturday school lived in Moss Side, Hulme, Whalley Range and Old Trafford. Pamela, who lived elsewhere, said that as well as her mother's involvement with Abasindi she was motivated to go to Saturday school because, unlike the predominantly White secondary school she attended, there was no racism:

> ... I felt safe in Moss Side. At Saturday school I was with safe people. People that, although they told you off or told you to do things, it wasn't for their benefit it was more for yours. So they pushed you for you, rather than pushing you for them. I learnt a lot about culture and Black history, which made me stronger in Wythenshawe. If you know what I mean, it gave me that backbone for Wythenshawe, to stand up for my rights and to know that I was somebody.
>
> (Pamela)

Jennifer, who lived with her parents in the North of England, said that her experiences of racism at infant school were not restricted to dinner ladies ignoring children or chanting 'black sambo', but also occurred within the classroom. As the only Black child in the class she not only had to listen to golliwog stories but also to the headteacher's version of the origins of Black people. In the words of the headteacher, 'Black people were black because when God made them everybody had to run into the sea but Black people could only put their hands and feet in the water'. When she told her parents about this incident her mother did not hesitate to 'tell the teacher off'.

 Having failed in her attempt to get her secondary school to cater for the dietary needs of not only Asian but Black children, Doretta approached her headteacher regarding the wearing of white socks as part of the school uniform. She felt that in the school photograph the Black girls looked as though they were wearing plaster of Paris. She showed the photograph to the headteacher and asked if it would be possible for the girls to wear black or brown socks. The headteacher agreed to raise the issue with the education department. Doretta said that in the meantime:

> I decided to get other girls to back this petition and we rallied together but most of the girls laughed at me saying 'gosh you are such a Moss Side gal', but that didn't stop me. It must have been a few weeks later when the Head came back and said 'looks like you've won this one as from next term all girls will be able to wear brown, black or grey socks as part of their uniform'. I felt a sense of victory.

The internal dialogue stage in the DAISE model includes reflection and critical exploration of similarities and differences between personal cultural practices and those of the dominant group. Melanie observed that the Saturday school's replacement of meaningless Eurocentric nursery rhymes with powerful mantras such as, 'we are the children of mother Africa, you better clear the way let we pass', made her felt connected to her ancestors. The penultimate, self-acceptance, stage of the DAISE model is similar to the last stage of Phinney's (1990) ethnic identity achievement. For the children at Abasindi Saturday school, this stage was represented by pride and a sense of belonging.

When Melanie, at the age of 9, was told by a White boy at her primary school in Moss Side to 'go back to her country', she took responsibility for organizing the Black Friday protest, seeing it as a natural response to the racist comment. This was also an opportunity for her to share her knowledge of Africa with the other children and she felt proud and confident that she was being listened to: 'I had a positive sense of self and I was not about to give it up, especially when told to go back to my country, knowing this is also my country'.

In her 2001 study, Blackburn identified ages 6 to 9 as the period when Black children become aware of their difference and are consciously involved in finding out more about their heritage. Externalization is the final stage of the DAISE model, and Abasindi gave children and young people the space to develop the knowledge and skills to enable them to engage confidently with their cultural heritage, both within the community and the wider society.

Doretta's decision that the West African dance routines she learnt at Abasindi should form the basis of Black girls' performance in the school multicultural talent show is but one example of this confident engagement. Although her friends thought she was crazy, she said that she wanted to bring the rhythms and beats of something that represented her as a Black girl. The girls' contribution to this event was a great success and it was the talk of the school for months. It also opened the doors to other Black girls venturing into Moss Side and joining Abasindi.

> **CHRISTINE EDWARDS**
>
> I can clearly recall the day my auntie was having the conversation with my mum about me attending Abasindi Saturday School. I was a very shy and reserved child and had no wish to attend Saturday School. All I was told was that I would be attending the following Saturday, other Black children would be attending and it would aid my education, end of conversation. Anyone who was a young person during the '70s or '80s will remember we had no say in our parents' decision making. Don't get me wrong – we were loved but it was just that generation's way. But as a child I did find living in Britain and being a Black child confusing and challenging.
>
> It was decided I would go to Abasindi with my younger brothers. My parents were quite lenient about my brothers' attendance, but I was made to attend religiously. I clearly remember being anxious and afraid the night before my first visit, being concerned and asking myself the questions: Would I fit in? Would the teachers be kind? Would I understand the work, let alone be able to complete it? My shyness made me so worried about having to mix with other young people.
>
> On arrival the teachers were welcoming and one of the first things I noticed was that all the teachers were Black. Initially I hated going and resented the fact that I had to give up my Saturday mornings. But I always ensured that I was obedient and worked hard and over time I did make several friends and academically began to excel. Over time my feelings changed. Let me explain that the Abasindi lessons were delivered by strong, educated and articulate Black women, yet they were so caring and patient. Their knowledge was vast, yet they were

still so humble; any egos were left at the Abasindi front door. I learnt the true importance of education, history and, for me the cornerstone, being steadfast in who I am and what I believe. Attending Abasindi I was challenged academically, personally and spiritually and I am so grateful for those experiences now, whereas at the time I thought I was being punished. The irony of it; ha ha!

One of the fundamental things I drew from my experiences with these women was their nurturing and teaching gave me the confidence and ability to be proud of my Black history, thrive academically and most importantly to truly know myself. On reflection attending the Abasindi has been one of the most powerful and empowering things I have experienced.

You may not think it is , but growing up as a child in Britain during the late '70s and '80s was very disempowering. Black people were systematically marginalized – being Black you were made to feel like a second-class citizen, and being female to know your place, and that was fundamentally in the home. My experience attending Abasindi showed me how to be strong, realize my dreams and not let anyone dictate who I am. I am grateful and in debt to all these women who reached me and touched my life in so many ways. They took my hand and replaced my shyness with confidence. My fear of failure they replaced with the belief I can succeed. Where I had self-doubt they nurtured and gave me the ability to see I am one of God's children. They educated and taught me to be the strong confident woman that I am today. Looking back, just to think I thought I was getting a raw deal having to attend Abasindi while my brothers could opt out; I now understand it was my brothers who got the raw deal.

Abasindi and the Louise Da-Cocodia Education Trust

The late Louise Da-Cocodia declared that one of the reasons for her voluntary work in the community was to 'help young Black people understand that this is their home, this is the society they live in, and that they have a part to play in developing it'. Members of Abasindi are now actively involved in the organization and development of the Louise Da-Cocodia Education Trust

Marsha White, Mellisa White and Beverley Hypolite – children of the Abasindi Summer School

Supplementary Education programme. This entails a weekly Saturday School and the Getting Ahead Cultural and Personal Development programme. As a strategy for increasing representation, between 2000 and 2005 and funded by Cariocca Enterprise, the Trust administered a small grants programme for African-Caribbean heritage students who were enrolled on college and university courses in accountancy, science, engineering, information technology, business enterprise, occupational therapy, medicine and dentistry. This work was extended and the pilot projects included the Raising Education Study Skills Project (RESPECT), the Parenting Advocacy Support Service (PASS), Developing Inclusive Community Education (DICE), the Raising Educational Attainment Cultural Heritage Project (REACH), our Moss Side Video Project, the Barriers Access and Gaps Project and the RISE Project for Black boys at risk of exclusion from school.

Sowing seeds of success

Louise Da-Cocodia and Elouise Edwards (left) and Betty Luckham (right) were founding members of Cariocca Enterprise and Arawak-Walton Housing Association

The Louise Da-Cocodia Education Trust Saturday Supplementary School was a direct outcome of Edwards-Kerr's 2005 study, 'Understanding the educational needs of African-Caribbean young men and developing pathways for action'. This study was undertaken in response to persistent underachievement, school failure and the disproportionate number of school exclusions among African-Caribbean heritage pupils, particularly boys. In comparison to other pupils, Black boys and girls of African-Caribbean heritage who participated in this study said they lacked a sense of 'belonging'. Unlike White pupils, they nevertheless believed in the value of schooling in preparing them positively for the future. Of the 93 Black pupils aged 12–15 from five Manchester secondary schools, 26 per cent said that they have had fixed-term exclusions. Black boys were more likely to be in detention than any of the other groups. Edwards-Kerr (2005) argued that this combination of exclusion and under-attainment often meant that Black men who entered university did so at an older age and were likely to be under-represented in certain career areas and over-represented in community work courses.

The Louise Da-Cocodia Education Trust Saturday Supplementary School focuses on providing a learning and teaching environment that encourages individual and team work, so developing a 'can do' approach to new experiences in its students. In a survey to ascertain why parents sent their children to Saturday School, most said that it was to help with their schoolwork and to prepare them for high school. One parent commented: 'We must be honest about things; our kids are failing when they get to high school. We need all the resources available to help them'. Parents expressed relief that their children were in a safe and happy learning environment. Some of the parents were keen for their children to learn about African-Caribbean history and African-Caribbean cuisine, as this would not only introduce the children to their cultural heritage but would also enhance their sense of pride and self-worth. The routine and structure of attending the Trust Saturday School had also developed their children's self-discipline and encouraged rapport between children and their parents.

In the study on *Aspiration and Engagement: Strategies for working with young Black men* (Davis et al., 2012), young people, community workers, parents and youth workers in Moss Side and Hulme pointed to the important role of families and the home as a source of reinforcement, particularly in relation to educational opportunities. Praise and encouragement, and the celebration of the achievements of young people were regarded as crucial to their development. However, some students faced a dilemma over balancing their parents' expectations with those of the school. One of the community workers gave an example of a boy whose parents wanted him to be an engineer whereas the school advised him to pursue a career in sports. This created a conflict between the school and the parents. The boy opted to go with the school's advice, believing that the school was better placed to assess his abilities. Here the young person conforms to the traditional institutional stereotyping and to a belief in the school's better position to determine the future of its pupils. The widely held stereotypical view of Black pupils as good at sport, rather than academic echoes the experiences of the poet Benjamin Zephaniah (2005) during the 1960s, and the 28-year-old man who stated that:

> ... I don't know if it was just because of the colour of my skin or the fact that all Black people are meant to be good at sport but they physically, literally forced me to play every sport in the school even like I never played cricket before, I got good, never played rugby before, I got good.

Several parents observed that the Saturday School had exposed their children to an environment where there were Black teachers as role models to boost confidence and motivation. The REACH report (2007) recommended that Black boys and their teachers be introduced to 'positive Black male role models who can engage, support and empower vulnerable Black boys and young Black men to turn their lives around ...', defining a role model 'as someone you look up to and respect and someone who impacts your life in a positive way' (REACH, 2007: 24). In Manchester, the Strategy to Elevate People (STEP) project and the City College Manchester Mentoring Programme were aimed at enabling inner-city young people to identify with positive images of success beyond the entertainment industry and sports.

As a follow-up to Edwards-Kerr's study, the research by Davis *et al.* on *Aspiration and Engagement: Strategies for working with young Black men* (2012), focused on issues relating to young people's aspirations. The research was specifically linked to the work of the Louise Da-Cocodia Education Trust and other community and voluntary sector organizations in Moss Side and Hulme. A total of 17 young people and 16 adults took part in the research. The adults included youth and community workers, community activists, volunteers and an adult education tutor. All the participants expressed the view that parents should be at the forefront of instilling an education mindset in their children. The young people also acknowledged that they valued education as a result of values that were instilled in them at an early age. One woman said that she was actively involved with her son's education up to university level, and this included meeting with his lecturers from time to time. Although it was important for parents to understand the educational system, their expectations and attitude were regarded as equally important.

Evidence suggested that the careers services were not putting young people's aspirations at the centre of the decision-making process. As a consequence, young people are leaving school without attaining the necessary qualifications to fulfil their career aspirations. Similar to the findings of Edwards-Kerr's 2005 study, a number of young people were doing courses that were not necessarily linked to their employment aspirations and personal development. One of the youth workers was of the opinion that:

> ... nobody is actively listening to the young people and finding out what they are interested in. They are doing what they think is best for them, finding out what they are interested in and putting

> those into place might be a key element in education, employment and training and getting them involved.
>
> (Davis *et al.*, 2012: 19)

From discussions with the young people it was evident that they were investing a lot of time and effort in studying subjects that they felt were irrelevant to their future careers and existing employment opportunities. They were doing so in the belief that:

> The more qualifications you get the more you can put on your CV for experience. So if you are applying for any job it's what is on your CV that will get you that job. If you have loads of qualifications on the CV then you are most likely to get the job and that's what I'm interested in.
>
> (Davis *et al.*, 2012: 19)

The research further established that young Black men often have higher educational and career aspirations than some of their peers, but that aspirations are affected by changes in their lives related to conditions around them. These include peer pressure and the lack of relevant services to meet their needs. However, the research also provided evidence that positive peer relationships contribute to young people continuing in further education. The young people in the study by Davis and colleagues stated that it was this sense of camaraderie that helped them to remain engaged with their studies.

Based on their classroom experiences, some of the boys in Javed's 2012 study echoed the views of parents that it was important to have more Black teachers in mainstream schools. Javed's study revealed that Black boys believed that Black teachers understood them and were less likely to treat them in a stereotypical manner. The Runnymede Trust (1997: 19) found that 'African Caribbean students frequently experience relationships with White teachers that are characterised by relatively high degrees of control and criticism'. This finding has been replicated in infant and primary classrooms. Ironically, the percentage of teachers from Black and ethnic minority backgrounds fell from 11.6 per cent in 2008/9 to 11.2 per cent in 2009/10. Overall the teaching profession remains predominantly White. The Department for Education's School Workforce Survey (2011) found that 24 per cent of school-age pupils in England were of Black and ethnic minority heritage, but that there was serious under-representation of minority ethnic teachers in every sector (Hick *et al.*, 2011). Richard Majors' Teacher Empathy programme aims to identify and develop those inter- and intra-personal skills teachers need in order to create effective relationships with young people in a positive climate for learning. Such skills include the ability to communicate more effectively, raise attainment, manage difficult behaviour, find alternative solutions to punishments and exclusions, and reduce stereotyping and unfair treatment.

Brenda McDonald teaching at the Saturday School

Javed (2012: 14) found that despite experiences of racism, success and achievement for the boys in his study entailed 'having ambition, finishing school, getting good grades, being in a secure job and having the opportunity to support family'. In her discussion on 'spaces of possibility' bell hooks argued that:

> The academy is not a paradise, but learning is a place where paradise can be created. The classroom with all its limitations, remains a location of possibility. In that field of possibility we collectively imagine ways to move beyond boundaries, to transgress. This is education as the practice of freedom.
>
> (hooks, 1994: 207)

However, placing boys in lower sets because of their behaviour can have an adverse impact on their future education and employment opportunities: 'I've got better marks than half the guys in the top set but they're like na: we, don't think you're ready and your behaviour needs to improve and that's rubbish'. The boys also spoke about their experiences of overt racism:

'There's this fat teacher who said to me that she might be fat but at least she's not Black' (Javed, 2012: 41–4). Article 2 of the United Nations Convention on the Rights of the Child states that:

> We shall respect and ensure the rights set forth in the UN Convention to each child without discrimination of any kind, irrespective of the child's or his or her parent's or legal guardian's race, colour, sex, language, religion, political or other opinion, national, ethnic or social origin, property, disability, birth or other status.
>
> (United Nations, 1990: 46)

A number of the boys in Javed's study openly acknowledged that they were viewed as rebels by their teachers: 'They would have seen us as rebels init because we're not following the school rules but if the school rule had an, if it had an explanation to why it was a rebellious thing or why it was wrong then alright, but if not then why not'. For these boys school was not viewed as a place of learning but rather a battleground to gain recognition (Majors, 2001). Sewell (1997) identifies four categories of Black boys: conformists, innovators, retreatists and rebels. The rebels are regarded as being opposed to the goals and means of schooling. This was not true of the boys in Javed's study – according to Sewell's categories, they were retreatist in that they accepted the goals of schooling but were opposed to its means. They also acknowledged the significance of support from their teachers and family members.

In their discussion of the role of family and kinship, Wright *et al.* (2010: 70) argue that the 'social and cultural capital of the Black family is often viewed by mainstream society as being weak and negative', particularly in the case of single female-led households. But this does not reflect the reality of the 25 year old who attributed his education and professional success to the women in his family: 'I come from a very strong matriarchal family that have instilled that strength in me ... There was not many male figures around when I was growing up. As a child it was predominantly women and that's where I get my strength from'. Another young man also declared that his decision to go to university was very much influenced by what Thomson *et al.* (2002) describe as 'critical moments'. He was referring to events seen as 'having important consequences', such as his desire to pay tribute to the memory of his late mother. Strand and Winston (2008) argue that African-Caribbean heritage young people start secondary school with aspirations of wanting to become doctors, pilots and lawyers but that aspirations are not static but dynamic, and consequently young people often change aspirations in the light of new experiences, maturity and sometimes parental influence.

Jumoke, Francia, Jennifer and Veronica at the Manchester Black Parents, Children and Young People Conference

Consistent with the aims of Saturday supplementary schools, some members of Abasindi played a key role in organizing the 2009 Manchester Black Parents, Children and Young People Conference. The conference was aimed at building an alliance between parents, teachers and communities and it intended to address issues of low qualifications and disproportionate school exclusions among particular groups of Black communities (Hick, 2010). The conference was organized in partnership with Manchester Metropolitan University and took place during Black History Month. In addition to two keynote speakers, Richard Majors and Gus John, local organizations took part, including the West Indian Centre Saturday Supplementary School, Mothers Against Violence, the Black and Asian Police Association, the Chrysalis Family Support Project and the founder of Universal Connection Soca Aerobic Ltd and former member of Abasindi, Esther Furlonge Clarke. This level of community engagement marked an important shift from 'papership' to 'partnership'.

Charles Critchlow observed that for him, as a representative of the Black Police Association, the conference was an opportunity to work in partnership with practitioners in the field of education and community development. His decision to facilitate the workshop on Exclusion and the Criminal Justice System was influenced by his concerns about the patchiness of social justice. The importance of addressing issues that are likely to impact positively on the educational experiences of Black young people was evident in the workshops on Motivating Learning Through Students' Everyday Interests (Washington Alcott), 'Eagles That Soar' – Black Pupils Achieving Success (Lorna Roberts) and Space Exploration: Black Contributions to Aeronautics and the Space Programme (Conway Mothobi). Omena Osivemu and Paul Lewis were two of the young people that facilitated workshops, On the Transition from Primary to Secondary School and Music – How they work Together'. The workshop on building a culture of success offered participants:

> ... insights and understandings about educationally 'successful' minority ethnic pupils – who are often ignored and overlooked within the prevalent concerns with 'under-achievement'. Understanding academic success says a lot about under-achievement. The recognition and 'celebration of BME success provides an important challenge to the constant tirade of negative images and associations of BME young people as 'problem' and 'failing' pupils. Participants might be inspired to develop new, more positive ways of thinking about minority ethnic pupils, parents and issues of achievement.
>
> (Stirling, 2009: Section 3)

The Manchester Black Parents, Children and Young People Conference had several outcomes. One was the Barriers, Access, Aspirations and Gaps project, undertaken in partnership with Zion Arts Centre (Z-Arts) and one of the local youth centres in Old Trafford. Here storytelling was viewed as having significance as an art form and not as mere entertainment. Several of the 15 young people (aged 15 to 25 years old) in the project found storytelling to be a valuable communication and motivational tool. The sessions gave them the opportunity to reflect upon their educational experiences and aspirations. One of these girls remarked that it was the first time she had given any thought to career and educational aspirations: 'first time I've talked about the future, made me think about what I want to do in the future more seriously'. Engaging in a process that involved role play and poetry performances increased the confidence levels of some of the younger members of the group. The significance of informal educational sites as a source of information and knowledge was another emergent theme.

The findings of this project challenged the assumption that the low participation in further and higher education by young people in Moss Side, Hulme and Old Trafford was due to lack of aspiration and confidence. From the discussions it was apparent that the young people had high and varied aspirations. Some of them were knowledgeable about what was required to realize their ambitions, although most were not. Edwards-Kerr (2005) found that although Black pupils had high academic and professional aspirations and ambitions for the future, many of the young people were unclear as to the routes that were available for them or what was required for them to attain their career goals. She cited the case of the young person who wanted to be a solicitor but was instead enrolled on a travel and tourism course, and of another who wanted to do hairdressing but her college offered only drama and English.

At the 2013 conference, Making Education a Priority – Alternative Approaches, keynote speaker, Diane Abbot MP, spoke about the benefits of having more Black male teachers in the classroom. The 2012 research project 'Race Equality in Teacher Education' was aimed at exploring teacher educators' understanding of race in/equality issues within education and how they were addressing issues of race inequality within their practice. Diane Abbot emphasized the importance of Black Supplementary School. However, Kehinde Andrews (2013: 52) argues that the 'politics in the supplementary school movement is not always quite as radical or tied into global issues of Black liberation' as it should be. Furthermore these schools do not represent a mass movement of Black people in education, nor have they inspired parents to take collective action (John, 2006). As well as developing a greater interest in education, Saturday supplementary schools in Manchester can raise the aspirations of young people through their participation in this specific form of community based initiative (Pollard, 2011), a strategy Mirza argues has been 'used by parents to side-step the perpetual hum of racism' (2009: 57).

Education is a fundamental dimension of Black women's political activism and an 'important link between self, change and empowerment ...' (Collins, 1990: 47). The everyday experiences of these women form the basis of a culture of refusal and resistance by way of their engagement with all levels of the British educational system. The ongoing involvement of Abasindi members in a range of community-based education programmes is a testament to women's commitment to the individual and the collective advancement of the Black community.

Chapter 7
The politics of sisterhood

Introduction
This chapter briefly explores the juncture of feminist and anti-racist struggle on the fronts that came to characterize the politics of sisterhood within the Abasindi Cooperative: domestic violence, immigration controls, community support and Black women's educational advancement. Personal reflections on the role of the organization in social action on each of these areas are interwoven with a critical analysis of contemporary literature. The aim of the chapter is to highlight the ways in which the politics of sisterhood grew and morphed in response to the needs of the community in which it was located. As Gramsci and Hoare (1978) argued, theories of change must emerge from the everyday struggles that drive the need for social transformation; we were the women we fought for.

The type of sisterhood Abasindi engendered as they addressed the challenges that confronted Black women in the 1980s meant that though we espoused feminist values, we did not always describe ourselves as a feminist organization; we often found ourselves distanced by the seeming ethnocentricity of Western feminist ideas. Ours was a kind of feminism that grew with the organization; it was pragmatic and socially meaningful for our realities. For example, unlike many feminist groups, we built alliances with men who supported our objectives. This was not altogether unproblematic because there were times when androcentricity reared its head and we needed to reassert control, especially when it appeared that our agenda was being subverted to serve the interests of male authority.

We were influenced by a Pan-Africanist philosophy but we had no tolerance for the entrenched patriarchies that are intrinsic to women's oppression and the ways in which women's rights were often marginalized in Pan-Africanist discourse. We fought equally for women's rights, human rights and anti-racism. Chimamanda Ngozi Adichie writes in her novel *Americanah*, 'Race is not biology; race is sociology. Race is not genotype; race is phenotype' (2013: 337). As an organization of Black women we did not hold with imposed prescriptions of what it means to be Black; you worked this out for yourself. As Adichie says, race only matters because of racism.

The politics of sisterhood

Speakers at Black Women's Mutual Aid Conference

We collaborated with many other groups that shared our aims. So for example, although we were a secular organization, our recognition of the role of religion in the lives of the Black community meant that when a local church offered refuge to a political activist threatened with deportation to Sri Lanka, Abasindi readily aligned with its cause and became heavily involved in mobilizing support and fundraising. The issues we took on were local but our education was transnational, informed by visiting activists from South Africa, Palestine, Nicaragua, Angola, Mozambique and elsewhere. Our experiences of British colonialism (we all had our origins in countries that had been colonized by Britain) and the racial, gender and class inequalities we fought were underpinned by a form of socialist feminism (Brah, 1991), which challenged exploitation and discrimination in areas such as housing, criminal justice, women's rights, immigration, employment and education (Bryan *et al.*, 1985). We strategized, organized and protested around these issues at home and we joined in the campaigns for social justice abroad.

Were there dangers that in this eclectic approach Abasindi could lose its identity as a political organization of Black women? This might have happened but for the formal evaluations of the organization's achievements and the process of introspection and reflection that occurred organically as we embraced change. In 1979 for example, the organization (which was then known as the Manchester Black Women's Cooperative) undertook a critical appraisal and concluded there was need to embed the Cooperative more fully within the lives of local women and to expand its range of activities so as to be better able to address community needs. It was at this stage that the organization became the Abasindi Women's Cooperative. The extract from the report of this decision (Abasindi archive material, n.d.) reasserts the organization's stance as a self-determining body of Black women, autonomous and separate from the control and influence of men.

During the 1980s and 1990s Abasindi's presence in the local community grew, as physical as it was political. We controlled our own representation and external recognition of what we stood for was enough to cement our identity even as we transmuted over time. We were not interested in establishing a reified version of Abasindi, or of sisterhood, feminism or anti-racism; we took the position articulated by Lather:

> The task of counter-hegemonic groups is the development of counter-institutions, ideologies and cultures that provide an ethical alternative to the dominant hegemony.
> (Lather, 1984, cited in Weiler, 2009: 226)

I am my sister's keeper: Combining the personal, the political *and* the professional

As women of Abasindi we had our personal lives, our political lives and our professional lives and for many of us the boundaries between these spheres of life were permeable; we carried our roles and perspectives like rucksacks from one to the other. The Abasindi women who worked in the field of immigration advocacy were very likely to have someone in their family who was affected by immigration controls; the women who worked in higher education were there because they had witnessed, often in respect of their own children, the under-harvesting of ability among Black boys in the school system that would thwart their opportunities later on; the psychologist, social worker or counsellor who was a member of Abasindi is likely to have observed the over-representation of Black children in care, or of Black people in mental health institutions, and those with law degrees often became the seekers of justice in racial harassment or criminal justice cases that blighted their neighbourhoods. For some of these women Abasindi had helped to chart their course to success and though there was no obligation, it became the way of things that one should offer whatever skills and knowledge one had acquired to support others:

> It was the first request I'd received for social work support outside of my role as a professional social worker with a local authority. The family of four children was headed by a single-parent woman and lived in a cramped council flat in a socially deprived area notorious for high levels of crime; there was racism too – racist graffiti greeted them many mornings. The mother, Ayesha (not her real name) was a qualified accountant but hadn't been able to get work in her field and did two cleaning jobs; her eldest child, age 16, was also working to bring in some money. The family was from West Africa, but most of the children were born in the UK and, cooped up on the sixth floor, they were as rambunctious as any. The flat was clean and tidy but carried the hallmarks of poverty: mismatched carpet squares, over-washed school shirts with threadbare collars force-dried over radiators for wear again tomorrow, patched up wallpaper and curtains too thin to offer more than a pretence of privacy. It was home. I was from a West African family myself and had spent part of my childhood in a council maisonette; this could have been my home and what bound me to them was the fact that like us, the family was determinedly father-less.
>
> The mother of these children had lived for a very long time as a victim of her husband's violence, and so had mine. Bruised eyes, dark glasses, blood and broken bones were the physical manifestations of a psychological terror we lived with all the time, that he could and would erupt without notice or provocation – as children, we learned to creep about like Jack, silently so as not to waken this fearsome giant. The emotional tension was so intense that it was almost with a sense of relief we ran to hide when he did start to hit out, under beds, in cupboards or squashed thin against the wall, holding your breath to make yourself invisible. The relief quickly gave way to a pounding terror, as the sounds and sights of mum being punched and kicked pervaded the house – there was no way to hide from this.
>
> To this day, some 50 years later, the memory invokes the rising vomit I had to fight to hold back as a small child. Ayesha's family, like ours, had finally escaped the violence and were now father-

less. We never thought about the good a father might bring to his children, we had no experience of this; for us being without a father simply meant being without his violence and as I sat in the council flat on that first meeting, I felt the sanctity of the safety of this cramped little place as keenly as I had in our maisonette. The family had been housed from a women's refuge by the council, Ayesha's husband did not know where they were living and it was crucial he didn't find out.

And this is where our narratives take a different shape. Leaving my father meant my mother could raise her children in relative peace but for Ayesha, leaving a violent husband had catapulted her into virtual statelessness and this created a whole set of different threats for her and her children. Despite having lived in the UK for over 14 years she was not a citizen and her right to stay was tied to her status as the wife of someone with a British passport. She divorced her husband and he reported her to the Home Office. Shortly after, she was issued with a deportation order. The Home Office (now the UK Borders Agency) was merciless; she was directed to leave the UK. Her council flat was taken as evidence of her dependency on the state and it was assumed that she would be a long-term drain on the welfare system should she be allowed to remain in the UK. The deportation order would have the effect of enforced separation from her children, three of whom were British citizens and could remain.

This was the 1980s and people subject to immigration controls were not officially restricted from accessing welfare support. However, since the 1960s, social security officers had been under 'secret internal instructions' to restrict benefits paid to 'any claimant who appears to come from abroad' (Kundnani, 2007a: 75). By 1988, new income support regulations had all but formally embedded immigration control and surveillance as part of the welfare state. Had Ayesha remained within a violent marriage, the family would have been entitled to apply for support from the state if they had been destitute but as a Black single mother of four children, without the right to live in the UK, her family was now facing institutionalized destitution. The use of the welfare system as a surveillance tool was later reinforced by the Asylum and Immigration Appeals Act 1993, which placed a duty on local authorities to investigate the immigration status of benefit claimants suspected of being asylum seekers and to pass the information on to the Home Office (Kundnani, 2007a).

Ayesha could not leave her children and, left with few choices, she decided to claim asylum. [This was before immigration rules changed to make it all but impossible to claim asylum once a person has entered the country.] She claimed that forcing her to leave would be in breach of rights laid down in the 1950 European Convention on Human Rights (ECHR). Her application was rejected. Ayesha had four children, three of whom were British citizens, a fact that was simply swept aside. Should Ayesha decide to leave them in England, then they would be taken into care. With staggering disregard for the best interests of the children, the Home Office contacted the local authority to alert them that a placement might be needed. It was at this stage that Ayesha came to Abasindi. Known for its social and political activism against injustice to Black women, Ayesha's situation represented two of the most pressing issues of the 1980s with which the organisation was grappling: domestic violence and immigration control. Over three decades later, the political and economic landscape may have changed but the double danger Black women face when they are caught up within violent relationships and subject to immigration control has not diminished. As it had done on behalf of many other women, Abasindi launched an anti-deportation campaign for Ayesha.

It was to be a long battle and though Ayesha eventually won the right to remain in the UK, the chronic stress and anxiety she suffered over the years it took exacted a huge toll on her health. Abasindi helped Ayesha to access free legal advice through one of its members, whose expertise on the subject led to her employment as an advice worker with an immigration rights agency, while in my role as social worker, I provided evidence in support of the needs and rights of the children to remain with their mother. Abasindi women collected petition signatures outside shopping and community centres, they engaged religious leaders, enlisted the support from the schools the children attended, leafleted government departments, harangued politicians, and held fundraising events to generate income for the family.

(Adele, Abasindi Member)

Abasindi Women (Abina, Joy and Shirley) at a vigil in Manchester

Simultaneous, multiple and interlocking oppressions: Domestic violence, immigration controls and poverty

Ayesha was much more than the sum of her experiences: she was resourceful, well-educated, ambitious and multi-skilled and she did not fit the image of the wounded and disempowered battered woman that pervades much of the domestic violence literature. Yet subject to 'simultaneous, multiple and interlocking oppressions' (Mann and Grimes, 2001: 8) the intersectionalization of these factors fed into a construction of an identity that demeaned these strengths: she was a poor, Black woman and what is more, as an African woman without resident status in the UK, she was, according to the dehumanizing surveillance of the Home Office, an alien subject. Though domestic violence is a universal problem, levels of risk are not universal: poor Black women 'are more likely to be in both dangerous intimate relationships and dangerous social positions' (Richie, 2000: 1,136), and women with temporary immigration status are particularly vulnerable as they are often unable to access welfare support that might facilitate their escape. Their immigration status might prevent them taking action against their partners in case they lose their right to remain in the UK (Gower, 2013). The common thread that runs through the wealth of research and literature on domestic violence is the recognition that this problem cuts across race, class, religion and nationality. Increasingly, however, scholars have questioned the ways in which the levelling out of differential experiences masked by universalizing statements such as this contributes to the marginalization of some women (Richie, 2000; Ristock, 2002; Russo and Pirlott, 2006). Abasindi's politics of sisterhood and the social action it spawned were based on a race and class analysis of violence against women that enabled differential risks and circumstances to surface.

Yes, domestic violence occurs in all settings but Ayesha's experiences were impacted by cultural and structural factors that meant she was exposed to threats that do not affect all women. Though there are high levels of domestic violence in many countries, Ayesha originated from a country in which domestic violence has long been viewed as a culturally rooted problem that is either too complex or not severe enough to warrant attention. This situation is as much a reality today as it was when Ayesha left Nigeria in the 1980s (International Rescue Committee, 2012). A 2014 article in 'Think Africa Press' reported:

> Between half and two thirds of Nigerian women are subject to domestic violence in their homes. This trend occurs across much of the world, but Nigeria's discriminatory laws and dismissive police compound its particularly high rates of domestic violence. Most potently, its prevalent culture of silence and stigma for the victims of domestic violence hinders public acknowledgement of the problem ... In general, domestic violence is seen as a 'private' matter to be dealt with by the family, typically a domain of male authority. Nigerian women are expected to behave with subservience to their husbands, and domestic violence is often accepted as a part of marriage. According to Amnesty International, many believe that a woman is 'expected to endure whatever she meets in her matrimonial home', and to provide 'sex and obedience' to her husband, who has the right to violate and batter her if she fails to meet her marital duties ... Domestic violence in Nigeria is often viewed as a necessary corrective tool for women, at best a part and parcel of married life.
>
> (Folami, 2013)

Although this article reports on Nigeria, it reflects values that have existed throughout history and in other countries, constraining women's agency and forcing them into acquiescence with patriarchal domination. Ayesha did not escape cultural constraints when she moved to live in the UK, and leaving her husband, though an act of resistance essential to her wellbeing, is likely to have led head-on into her having to confront other ways in which discourses of culture and the behaviours they engender can further bind women. Writing about the trauma of domestic violence, Nixon and Humphreys (2010) suggest that:

> To hold traumatic reality in consciousness requires a social context that affirms and protects the victim and that joins victim and witness in common alliance. For the individual victim, this social context is created by relationships with friends, lovers, and family.
>
> (Nixon and Humphreys, 2010: 137)

What is missing from this statement is the recognition that the common alliance may be severed if the victim takes a stand against oppressive cultural values that are part of the social context. Leaving a violent husband can result in a woman literally being jettisoned into cultural and social isolation, especially if she is viewed as having betrayed the conventions of domesticity to which the family and community subscribe. Nixon and Humphreys (2010: 138) go on to say that at the societal level the social context is created by 'political movements that give voice to the disempowered', but these movements can only be effective if their analysis of domestic violence also focuses on its cultural as well as its structural underpinnings. Abasindi women were acutely aware that, as Sokoloff and Dupont (2005) point out, the manifestations of domestic violence may differ according to cultural context. After all, the community in which the organization was located is still the most diverse in the region, with over 78 languages spoken in its schools (Daycare Trust, 2011). Abasindi was equally vociferous, however, in its rebuttal of the ready supply of simplistic and reductionist cultural arguments that, under the guise of 'cultural sensitivity', too often resulted in women being abandoned to their fate.

Discourses of culture – the embedded, and often implicit or tacit beliefs about what is normal or acceptable behaviour or ideas in a particular reference group (Fook and Askeland, 2007: 3) and about which there is a vast amount of literature (see for example the rich body of work by the cultural theorist Stuart Hall) – suffer from a dualism of objectivism and constructivism. On the one hand, the term is imbued with concretized notions of exotic artefact, behaviour or tradition and on the other, these 'objects' of culture are dependent upon subjective interpretation of meaning. When culture is served up as explanation for oppression or as justification for not intervening when women or children are at risk, the ambiguity

The politics of sisterhood

generated by this dualism is appropriated, whether inadvertently or not, to suppress the needs of marginalized communities. Though Ayesha *did* receive the support of a women's refuge, this is not something that she, as a Nigerian woman, could have taken for granted. A 2014 study of survivors of domestic violence from minority ethnic communities in the UK found that these women's access to services was restricted because of racism and cultural assumptions:

> Discourses of both cultural specificity and generality/ commonality are shown to intersect to effectively exclude minority ethnic women from such services. Domestic violence emerges as something that can be overlooked or even excused for 'cultural reasons', as a homogenized absence; or alternatively as a pathologized presence, producing heightened visibility of minoritized women both within and outside their communities – since domestic violence brings them and their communities under particular scrutiny.
>
> (Burman *et al.*, 2004: 332)

We do not argue here for the isolation of cultural factors in explaining domestic violence or in examining the responses of agencies; such an approach would limit understandings of diversity to privileged spheres of knowledge (Andersen and Collins, 2001). Neither do we argue that gender should be the primary basis of analysis. Instead we support the views of scholars such as Sokoloff and Dupont (2005), who have called for the examination of how 'other forms of inequality and oppression, such as racism, ethnocentrism, class privilege and heterosexism, intersect with gender oppression' (2005: 39). Such analysis should include the critical scrutiny of culture, not as exoticized characterization of the other, but of the ways in which discourses of culture are used to sustain hierarchies of interests and needs (Andersen and Collins, 2001). This might help to explain why women from ethnic minorities in the UK who are subject to domestic violence are rendered less visible, and their experiences explained away for cultural reasons (Burman *et al.*, 2004).

In 1989, around the same time as Ayesha won her right to remain in the UK, Amina Mama published her research on the statutory and voluntary sector responses to domestic violence against Black women. *The Hidden Struggle: Statutory and voluntary sector responses to violence against Black women in the home* turned the spotlight onto the institutions and structures that were designed to help: the criminal justice system, housing services, police and social services, refuges and voluntary organizations. Mama's research revealed extensive failings of policy and practice and demonstrated the ways in which entrenched structural inequalities compounded problems for women escaping violence if they were Black. The strategy adopted by Abasindi in its support of women involved building anti-violence coalitions based on a view of violence grounded in intersectionality that recognized these inequalities (Collins, 1998).

Though the organization took a general stand on violence against women, we saw that women were not equally affected by violence. For example, had Ayesha been a Black British or White woman, leaving a violent husband would not have resulted with her facing forced removal from the country or separation from her children. Intersectional analysis also reveals that poor women are at greater risk of violence in the home because they have fewer resources to draw on to ensure their safety. And Black women are more likely to be in poverty than White women (except for women from traveller communities who also experience disproportionate poverty and structural disadvantage) (Singh and Webber, 2013). Families from Black and minority ethnic groups on average live on less than 60 per cent of the median UK household income (Singh and Webber, 2013). Had Ayesha been a woman of Caribbean descent escaping domestic violence, she might have been among the 30 per cent classified as income poor, a better position than women of African descent, for whom the rate is 45 per cent, and significantly better than had she been Pakistani (55 per cent) or Bangladeshi (65 per cent). These figures compare to the lowest rates of income poverty among White British people of 20 per cent (Palmer and Kenway, 2007).

As a lone-parent family – a prevalent family type in African and Caribbean communities in the UK -- a Black woman's risks of poverty increase considerably. And as an asylum-seeking family, the policy of enforced destitution that is a feature of current immigration policy may do exactly that: force them into destitution. One third of people who apply for asylum in the UK each year are women. This number has remained fairly constant for the past decade; in 2010, for example, 5,329 women claimed asylum compared to 12,571 men (Home Office, Immigration Statistics, April to June 2011: Asylum, Table as.03: Asylum applications from main applicants by age, sex and country of nationality.) The vast majority of asylum seekers live in poverty as they are unable to seek permission to work unless they have waited more than 12 months for a decision on their application, and during this time they do not have access to the social welfare system. Asylum seekers *can* apply for asylum support from the UK Border Agency, but the money they receive if they can prove destitution is set below subsistence level. Around 70 per cent of women's asylum claims are rejected and the situation for these women is particularly acute as they have no entitlements at all. Women subject to immigration controls are among the most disempowered of all groups in the UK. Their movement and civil liberties are controlled by the state and although they are unable to access welfare support, the irony is that the immigration system actually creates and enforces their dependence on the state (Cohen, 2006; Dumper, 2005). Before the deportation order, Ayesha was working and supporting her family but as a 'failed asylum seeker' she was not permitted to work and her restricted access to benefits meant the family had to live at below national subsistence levels. These differences show that it is not just race, class and gender that determine women's oppression, but institutional structures and equity of access to support.

Abasindi's political position was to take social action beyond the boundaries of culture, race, gender and class by confronting and even circumventing the systems which sustain these inequalities. For example, with women who were subject to immigration controls, one of our members helped them access one of the best free legal services available through the Greater Manchester Immigration Advice Unit. Good legal advice is essential for the protection of human rights and has long been a cornerstone of asylum advocacy work, yet cuts in services, alongside legal aid reforms, have led to a drastic reduction in the number and quality of immigration specialists. In 2010 Refugee and Migrant Justice was shut down, and in 2011 the Immigration Advisory Service was closed. The Greater Manchester Immigration Aid Unit (GMIAU), one of the oldest legal advice services in the country – and, incidentally, the agency that supported Ayesha in the 1980s – had a 70 per cent cut in funding for its legal aid work (Singh and Webber, 2013: 4). Together with cuts in services, legislative and policy changes have curtailed people's access to effective legal representation and although legal aid funding can still be obtained in asylum cases, general immigration work has been removed from the scope of legal aid. Cuts in services have differential impacts and, as women's immigration cases tend to be especially complex, women are disproportionately affected by these changes. The Institute of Race Relations summarizes the impact of these changes:

> ... the effects of the changes are injustice, destitution, illegal working, frustration, loss of faith in the justice system, desperation and exploitation. Many law firms have pulled out of asylum and immigration work altogether, or have significantly reduced the amount of work they are able to take on.
>
> (Singh and Webber, 2013: 3)

Alongside these challenges there have been some important advances in respect of women's rights. For example, the combined efforts of anti-violence and asylum advocacy campaigns resulted in changes to the immigration rules so that the spouse or partner of a person with British citizenship or resident status can now apply to stay in the UK permanently if she is a victim of domestic violence. In the past, the 'no recourse to public funds' rule prevented victims of domestic violence from accessing housing or welfare benefits until they had an immigration status that entitled them to public funds, such as 'indefinite leave to remain'. As few refuges would accept people without access to benefits, women often had no choice but to remain in the violent situation. In April 2012, however, a new policy concession was announced to enable women to apply for temporary immigration status, which gives access to public funds while they are waiting for a decision on their application for indefinite leave under the domestic violence rules.

Despite these positive changes, the fact remains that women like Ayesha still cannot access legal aid for representation if they have been issued with instructions that mean they must leave the UK and their children behind, or if their immigration status puts them at risk of being returned to a situation of violence or abuse. In this respect, things are worse now than they were 30 years ago. The government position that 'immigration is a matter of choice, so that those seeking to enter or stay should fund their own legal appeals' (Singh and Webber, 2013: 7) fails to take into account the specific risks that women face and ignores repeated calls for a gender-sensitive approach to immigration support (Dumper, 2005).

We met Ayesha in the early 1980s, but clearly domestic violence, poverty and immigration controls continue to restrict women's rights and freedoms today. Abasindi was one of the first organizations in the UK to address immigration controls, domestic violence and poverty as an interconnected human rights issue, an approach subsequently adopted by organizations such as 'Safety 4 Sisters Northwest', which points out on its website that 'a good service can be measured by its capacity to fulfil the needs of the most marginalised and vulnerable groups' and that has as its mission: 'Working towards securing greater protection, safety and support for women who have experienced gender violence and who have no recourse to public funds or state benefits' (Safety 4 Sisters Northwest, 2010).

Although set up primarily to support Black women, the Abasindi Cooperative acknowledged that alongside the specific concerns of women, marginalization and vulnerability were problems that affected the community more widely. In the 1980s, young Black people were being made increasingly vulnerable to long-term economic disadvantage and under-employment by an education system that was largely failing them (see Chapter 6), and a resurgence in racism, alongside the economic policies of the Conservative Government led by Margaret Thatcher, added to their marginalization. The UK had suffered a series of economic crises in the 1970s, and by the time Thatcher came to power in 1979, the country had joined the list of recession-hit countries in the economically developed world. Inflation was about 10 per cent and unemployment, which had been steadily increasing since the mid-1960s, reached record levels. By 1982, the number of unemployed had exceeded the 3 million mark, with people out of work being referred to as 'Maggie's millions' (BBC, 1982). The policy view at the time that the macroeconomic benefits of high unemployment outweighed its economic and social costs (Politics.co.uk, n.d.) seemed simply to consign young people in deprived areas to a future without hope (Lea and Young, 1982). It was only a matter of time before the simmering resentment and frustration that many people felt was to boil over; this was the backcloth to the 1981 riots. In the next section we turn our attention to these matters.

Supporting a community on fire

While Ayesha was battling violence in the home, violence erupted on the streets just a stone's throw away from where she lived. Abasindi Cooperative was housed in an old church building in the heart of Manchester's Moss Side community, an area where just over 50 per cent of the population are from Black or minority ethnic groups and where unemployment and deprivation were high. Evidence submitted to the Scarman Tribunal in the wake of the Brixton disturbances that preceded the eruption in Moss Side revealed that at the time young Black people encountered employment discrimination that thwarted their aspirations even when they had the qualifications for better jobs (Cross, n.d.). Even now, Moss Side is in the 1 per cent of the most deprived wards in the country and falls below national averages on most economic indicators. In 2007, the average unemployment rate was reported at 17 per cent, well above the city average of 9 per cent, while among one ethnic group, Somalis, unemployment was as high as 47 per cent. The high rate of unemployment among the Somali population of Moss Side is partly due to the fact that many are asylum seekers and are unable to work until their asylum application has been decided (Phillips *et al.*, 2007).

Back in 1981, it was 'Thatcher's Britain' and many young people felt disenfranchised, isolated and neglected. Racial tension was fuelled across the country by police harassment and the controversial 'sus' (stop and search) laws. The overt racism in the 1950s and 1960s had led to the growth of cultural and political resistance in the 1970s as ideas of Black consciousness and Black Power gained increasing popularity. Yet despite concerted anti-racist action and alliances, racism seemed not to be declining but increasing. With this as the backcloth, the 1980s' generation of young Black people in inner cities, trapped in worsening poverty, under-education and poor employment prospects, were ripe for protest. The death of 13 young Africans in a fire at a birthday party in New Cross in South London, suspected to be caused by racists, was the proverbial straw that broke the camel's back. A birthday party for a 16 year old ended in tragedy when the house was gutted, it was believed, through arson, in the early hours of Sunday 18 January 1981. A total of 14 young Black people lost their lives (the 14th died later in hospital) and a further 26 suffered serious injuries.

The government response at the time seemed to indicate an indifference to the loss of Black lives and this was exacerbated by a general belief that the police did not take seriously the possibility that the fire might have been caused by a racist firebombing. Later reports indicate that the fire had been caused by a faulty paraffin heater, but at the time the rise of racism and the increasing number of racist attacks pointed to racial hatred as the cause. When the focus of the investigation turned towards blaming the young people who had been at the party, there was outrage among the victims' families and local communities (La Rose *et al.*, 2011). A Black People's Day of Action was called. On 2 March 1981 around 25,000 people turned out on the streets of London to demonstrate against the general rise in racism and especially within policing practice. Abasindi was represented at the march by Diana Watt, Kath Locke, Elouise Edwards and Paula Jones.

Over the next few months the tensions mounted and violent unrest erupted right across the country, beginning in Brixton. By the end of the summer, there had been disturbances in Leicester, Birmingham, Preston, Blackburn, Sheffield, Newcastle, Luton, Wolverhampton, Stockport, Ellesmere Port, Liverpool, Chester and Manchester (La Rose *et al.*, 2011). In Manchester's Moss Side, both Black and White young people rioted, suggesting that it was not just racism, but also inner-city deprivation, that had fuelled the disorder. Reflecting on the events 30 years ago, people who had been present at the time commented:

> Buildings were being stoned and glass windows were falling apart. Buildings were burning. People were shouting and screaming. It was a cacophony of all those things. ... It was deeply concerning. There were particular concerns for the young people on the streets and the older people running around trying to find

their children. The riots were eventually brought under control but the conduct of some officers was heavily criticised. People who had done nothing wrong were indiscriminately arrested and assaulted ...

(Manchester Evening News, 2011)

Relations between the police and Black communities at the time could hardly have been worse. Professor John Rex observed that to 'catch each criminal youth it became normal practice to interview up to fifty others who by virtue of their blackness, their cultural symbols or suspicious behaviour, were thought to be possible criminals' (Rex, 1982: 101). Rex's comment might have been based largely on anecdotal evidence but statistics on the ratio of arrests and searches to actual convictions, and the rates of stop and search among different groups reveal that then, as now, criminogenic constructions continue to be influenced by racial stereotypes (Kundnani, 2007b). That policing practices were a key factor in the Moss Side riots perhaps explains why, during the height of the violence, the police station was besieged by angry crowds for three days. Father Phil Sumner, a Catholic priest who spent over 25 years working in Moss Side, described his recollections for the BBC:

> 'I turned the corner onto Quinney Crescent and there were hundreds of young Black people on one side and the police with their riot shields on the other,' he said. 'The next thing was, a brick bounced off the bonnet and hit the windscreen....I remember standing there talking when the police launched a baton charge into the crowd. We headed down what is now Raby Street, past Our Lady's Church, and at the gate was a burning barricade.'

> At the time, unemployment among young, black men in Moss Side had reached 80% and few stood a chance of finding a job. But it was the use of 'stop and search' by police that left many people in Moss Side 'waiting for something to happen'. 'The whole Black community – not just the young people – felt such anger towards the police', Father Sumner said. 'So there was a real breakdown in that relationship.' A memorable piece of graffiti at the time – 'Help the police, beat yourself up' – summed up the mood of many.

(Turner, 2011)

A local White physician, Donald Bodey, gave evidence to the Hytner Inquiry that followed the Moss Side riots. He told the inquiry that he was outraged at having to treat injuries caused by police brutality, injuries consistent with beatings, such as suspected fractured ribs, bruises and cuts on the face, legs and arms, and blood-filled cavities under the skin that he had 'never expected to see in England' (*New York Times*, 1981). Speaking out was, however, to exact a cost for Bodey and his wife as they subsequently became a target for racist extremists: 'We were also sent hate mail with razor blades in from far-right extremists', Carol Bodey told the *Manchester Evening News* (Glendinning, 2011).

Gender, race, class and protest

Variously called 'riots', 'protests', 'disturbances' and 'uprisings', depending upon one's political perspective, these events were the subject of numerous media reports, scholarly articles, books and government inquiry reports (the Hytner Report, 1981 and the Scarman Report, 1981). Reading through archive material from the time, one might be forgiven for thinking that gender was not a significant factor in the riots, that all the protagonists were male and all the women absent. That the outward face of the violence was male is undisputable, evident by the young Black men with their stones and bottles gathered on one side of the road and the policemen with their riot shields and truncheons on the other. But women were present. We were the mothers, sisters, girlfriends and grandmothers of the youths who had been failed by their second-rate education. We knew too many who had been shoehorned into unsatisfactory work training schemes, which offered no entry to 'the anterooms of employment' (Rex, 1982: 108) and, on the contrary, which only compounded their simmering frustration.

Women had been the ones to caution a respectful attitude to the police, the advice most Black inner-city parents issued to their children at some time, in the hope that this would prevent them being targeted. We had been witness when young people turned their discontent to the self-destructive pursuit of drug dealing and addiction; we were witness when they turned against one another in the violent gangs that troubled our neighborhood; and we had witnessed the ways in which the systematic neglect by the state had contributed to all of these problems. During the uprisings we saw evidence of the expression of particular masculinities that reified physical prowess and domination (Baker, 2009) and that disturbed us deeply. And through all of our witnessing we had observed the many young men and women of our communities who had risen above their adversities and were a credit to us all. Our witness was not passive but political. The great American writer James Baldwin declared himself 'witness to the truth' and wrote 'All over Harlem, Negro boys and girls are growing into stunted maturity, trying desperately to find a place to stand; and the wonder is not that so many are ruined but that so many survive' (Baldwin, cited in Blair, 2007: 178); we felt much the same way about the young people in Moss Side.

Despite our presence, any observations about the role of Black women were noticeably absent from the articles about the riots; a powerful lesson that we needed to be our own historians. The lack of a rigorous gender analysis does not mean, however, that discourses on the role of women (as mothers) or men (as fathers) did not surface in the post-mortem that followed. The hegemonic narrative that emerged, then as now, linked criminality with the deficits of parenthood and family. Female-headed single-parent households were held culpable for anti-government disorderly behaviour by young people, even in the face of glaring evidence about the extent of inequalities and social exclusion that such families experience (Ashe, 2014). Implicit in these discourses on single motherhood is another discourse, that of the missing father, the 'phantom' of Black family research, who has been studied more for his absence than his presence (Hill, 2003).

> A range of conservative commentators suggested that the aggression expressed by young men during the civil disorder was a product of absent fathers. Young men, they contended, need fathers to have a presence in their lives to reduce this kind of antisocial behaviour. These narratives depoliticised the causes of the civil disorder by depoliticising the constitution of the identities of those young men who participated in rioting and looting. They operated to sideline the role of socio-economic factors, including gender power relationships, in the production of young men's identities. Additionally, the depoliticisation of the riots through the narrative of the absent father framed the lone mother family as a failing family form.
>
> (Ashe, 2014: 654)

These observations, written in the aftermath of the disturbances of 2011, were also a feature of the analysis of those in 1981. However, those of 1981, despite negative press to the contrary, were not about single-parent families or the lawlessness of young people and Black communities. They were a reaction to the entrenched neglect of inner-city communities, a neglect institutionalized through government economic policy, and a reaction to attempts to construct Black people as aliens swamping the land in order to live off its welfare system (the irony being that the welfare system would have collapsed without Black people's taxes and labour).

The construction of the 'alien other' to serve nationalist and racist ideologies is understood as a process that has been institutionalized within societal structures at many levels. For example, a group within the Conservative Party – The Monday Club – published a pamphlet in 1981 that called for the repatriation of 50,000 immigrants each year, the abolition of the Commission for Racial Equality and the repeal of all race relations legislation. Harvey Proctor MP stated that the '"indigenous population" would only be reassured "that they are not, in the words of the Prime Minister, going to be swamped" if the size of the "ethnic population" was reduced to zero' (Runnymede Trust, n.d.). What Proctor and his bedfellows failed to appreciate was that the majority of the 'ethnic population' were British citizens, as were most of the people who had revolted against the rise of racist ideas such as this.

If the face of the violence in the events of 1981 was that of the young Black man, this too was understandable. The disturbances were fired by the racist and classist bias of the British education system, which disadvantaged Black boys in particular, and by policing practices that deliberately targeted and criminalized young Black men. There were multiple layers of structural disadvantage and though they concerned large swathes of people, Black and White and of all ages, who had been fighting race and class oppression for years, Black youth were at the nexus and felt the oppression more keenly than anyone. As Frost and Phillips (2011) put it, Black youth were not starting a fight, they were fighting back. In August 2011, trouble again broke out across the UK but the scale of the disorder was far greater than in 1981: the disturbances spread to 66 locations across the country, involved around 15,000 people, led to 4,000 arrests and cost five lives and an estimated half a billion pounds (Newburn *et al.*, 2011; Bridges, 2012). The social context was also somewhat different (Newburn, 2012). Though the spark for the initial protest in London was the killing of Mark Duggan, a Black man shot by a policeman, the antagonism that underpinned the disturbances that sprang up in other parts of the country was less about racism and more the result of generalized discontent.

The riots of 2011 differed from 1981 in other ways too; for example, they contained inflections of the consumerist preoccupations of British society, a factor not identified as a feature of the earlier uprisings. Furthermore, the instancy of the mobilization power of communication technology spread the unrest in ways that were not possible 30 years earlier. The disaffected were mobilized in days, whereas in 1981 there were three months between the initial incidents in Brixton and the protests in Moss Side. Mobile phones had served as a conduit not only for legitimate protest, but also for opportunism – some people seemed to join the fray not because of disadvantage, but to take advantage of the chaos. The disturbances in the summer of 2011 became a 'mix of violence, protest, looting and pleasure' (Ashe, 2014: 652) and the profusion of explanations that followed suggested their cause was the dysfunctionality of the single-parent family and 'moral vacuity, greed and popular culture' (Ashe, 2014: 654). Platts-Fowler (2013: 18) observed: 'The usual culprits cited as responsible for this breakdown were feral children whose parents had failed in their duty to socialise them, and criminal gangs', echoing views, such as those espoused by Carroll, that the disturbances were symptomatic of a 'spoilt brat mentality' linked to welfare dependency (Carroll, 2012, cited in Platts-Fowler, 2013: 18).

These explanations masked an inconvenient truth however. As in 1981, the history underlying the 2011 disturbances was the long-standing deprivation and neglect of certain sections of the population (Lea and Hallsworth, 2012; Wain and Joyce, 2012). Milburn's (2012: 402) argument that the riots emerged from a 'context of crisis and austerity' was supported by the fact that 70 per cent of those later brought before the courts were reported to have been from the 30 per cent most deprived areas in the UK (Ashe, 2014: 656):

> Young people, representing approximately half of riot participants (Ministry of Justice, 2012), had already been hit particularly hard by economic decline and austerity measures. Youth unemployment had reached record levels, and cuts to youth provision had left some young people with little to do ...
> (Platts-Fowler, 2013: 18)

The disturbances of 1981 were sparked by entrenched institutionalized racism plus structural disadvantage. In 2011, the most significant contextual factor seems to have been the demise of the welfare state and the harsh realities of neoliberalist policies (Kundnani, 2007b; La Rose *et al.*, 2011; Lea and Hallsworth, 2012; Milburn, 2012), which, not coincidentally, had their genesis in the period leading up to the 1981 events. Though less a protest about racism, what happened in 2011 revealed that racism in the police force was still a major concern (Solomos, 2011). Black people who had taken part in the riots reported unfair treatment at the hands of the police (Muir and Adegoke, 2011) and although there had been changes to the stop and search rules over the years, Black young people were still disproportionately targeted (Prasad, 2011). The police shooting of Mark Duggan, which had provoked the initial protest – a small and peaceful gathering of about 50 people outside Tottenham Police Station – revealed similar concerns about racist profiling within policing practice that had contributed to earlier disturbances.

There were also important gender considerations. In her analysis of riots that took place in 1991, Campbell (1993) highlighted the differential impacts of economic marginalization on men and women, while research into the 2011 riots by *The Guardian* and the London School of Economics (2011) revealed that gender was a factor in the shape and forms of disorder. We suggest that an analysis that explores the intersectionality of gender, class and race may reveal dynamics in the politics of resistance that might not be made visible by unitary approaches alone. For example, Ashe (2014) describes the violation to the sense of self that stop and search practices can evoke in young men who experience socio-economic exclusion (2013). Drawing on work by Messerschmidt (2000), Ashe posits that stop and search could be viewed as a 'very public form of emasculation' of one group of men by another more powerful group:

> Stop and search is not just an attack on the rights of the community; it is a technology that attacks the integrity of young men's identification with certain ideals of masculinities by invading their bodily space, discarding as irrelevant the traditional boundaries of male autonomy in the interests of surveillance. The issue of policing not only connects to class or racial politics but also incorporates a gender body politics.
>
> (Ashe, 2014: 659)

Given the dominance of repertoires of violence within discourses of masculinity (Barker, 2005), it is unsurprising that young men who believe they are victimized and marginalized use violence in their protests. After all, the behaviour of male police officers against which they are reacting draws on these same repertoires. While young men often resort to expressions of violence, Campbell (1993) noted that women are more likely to respond to their economic conditions by building community support. This too is hardly surprising. While violence is not necessarily a trait of masculinity, or peace of femininity, male violence is endemic within British society (Connell and Messerschmidt, 2005). Whether confronting police violence against their sons, or the gang violence that beset the Moss Side community for many years or, as we saw in the case of Ayesha, confronting domestic violence perpetrated against women by men, the Abasindi Cooperative had a long history of tackling violence, and had no appetite for more. The Abasindi strategy tended towards justice, support and strengthening community, rather than combat.

This was the primary role adopted by Abasindi in the Moss Side uprising of 1981. For example, the organization played an active part in supporting the Moss Side Defence Committee, which helped young people access legal advice and challenged the distortions in the media and police accounts of what had taken place. This spirit of solidarity was reflected right across the district as community services opened up their doors to support young people in the area. Under the leadership of community activists such as Charlie Moore, Hartley Hanley, Gus John, Beresford Edwards (Nana Bonsu), Paul Okojie, Ken McIntyre and others, support was provided to hundreds of young people, with two notable places of refuge being the Moss Side Youth Club and Hideaway. And as the fire raged, Abasindi became the place to which the injured were taken:

> ... community worker Elouise Edwards was helping to set up a makeshift hospital at the Abasindi centre to treat the injured. 'It was a terrible time,' she said. 'It was so frightening. One young White lad came in, he had been beaten up. He was an apprentice baker just coming home from his job; he didn't know what was going on. We took him to the hospital because his injuries were too big for us. We were Black people taking this young White man to hospital – we could have left him on the street – and he said something that has stuck with me forever. He said, "But you were the people they taught us to hate."'
>
> (*Manchester Evening News*, 2011)

> The day was not normal
> For days
> The air was static with tension
> It was feared expected and rejected as easily as breathing
> Hair weaves continued
> Cornrowing and stock checking
> African fabric and outfits
> Amongst the drums ready for rehearsals
>
> No Facebook or Twitter existed to newsflash
> But everyone knew it
> Heard it
> Smelt the fear felt the anger
> When all exploded at 2 a.m.
>
> This space
> This haven for women and children
> Now opened its arms to refugees
> Of local not global despair

>   Welcomed the injured
>   The frightened
>   This space gave solace and protection exactly when needed
>
>   One day, July 8th 24 hours
>   Two days, July 9th 48 hours
>   1981 Abasindi never closed its doors
>   To anyone
>   ('1981 Abasindi', SuAndi © 2014)

One of the responses to the disturbances of 1981 was to increase opportunities for Black people to enter further and higher education institutions through the establishment of access courses. In the next section we discuss the contribution of the Manchester Black Access Course to the politicization of Black women.

Accessing higher education

Although there have been improvements in the gender balance in higher education in that women now represent 44 per cent of academics in UK universities, the percentage of Black people remains disproportionately low at 1.6 per cent (Higher Education Statistics Agency, n.d.):

> At a recent public talk at University College London, titled 'Why Isn't My Professor Black?', black scholars claimed that insidious forms of racism may explain why just 85 of the UK's 18,500 professors are black, and only 17 are black women.
>
>   (Parr, 2014)

The racial inequalities these figures reflect have been the subject of research and policy concerns stemming from the riots of 1981 and even before. In 2009, the National Union of Students conducted a study of the gaps between the attainment levels of Black students and White. The survey of 938 respondents demonstrated that their experience of school and college had a direct impact on how a student performed in further and higher education settings and that coming from a poor socio-economic background, which was the experience for many Black people, had reduced their access during formative years to education of a standard that would equip them for adult learning. The report concluded that the attainment gaps would only be addressed through changing the organizational nature of institutions and tackling institutional racism, which they defined as:

> The collective failure of an organisation to provide an appropriate and professional service to people because of their colour, culture, or ethnic origin. It can be seen or detected in processes, attitudes and behaviour which amount to discrimination through unwitting prejudice, ignorance, thoughtlessness and racist stereotyping which disadvantage minority ethnic people.
>
> (The Macpherson Report, 1999, cited in National Union of Students, 2010: 56)

Alongside the need to tackle structural inequalities, some scholars believe there is also a need to establish accredited Black studies programmes within UK institutions. They point to the way the growth of women's studies over the last 30 years has contributed to knowledge on gender inequality and increased the visibility of feminist academics. It is argued that academia, while generating an impression that the production of knowledge is a neutral endeavour, is dominated by a Eurocentricity that marginalizes Black people's experiences and downplays the contributions of scholarship arising from the analysis of racial disadvantage. Gil Robinson claims that: 'Establishing black studies programmes will increase our visibility within universities and make the statement that our presence is worth studying, our presence is worth understanding and our contribution to this society, to academic life, to British life and to world life, is worth studying.' (Robinson, cited in Gabriel, 2013). Other commentators disagree and suggest that the capital of Black people in academic settings can only be fully utilized if they 'raise the presence and impact' of their academic output through research and publications (Davis, cited in Gabriel, 2013).

The call to increase the number of Black people in further and higher education settings has a long history and was given impetus after the 1981 uprisings, which it was believed stemmed in part from the inequities of the educational system (Rex, 1982) that not only prevented Black pupils from achieving their potential, but thwarted their access to higher education and satisfying employment. Black access courses were one of the measures instituted by Labour-controlled local education authorities in response to the Swann Report (1985), which had concluded that disadvantage among Black children resulted from a failure of the education system. Access courses were seen as a means of addressing this disadvantage and aimed to produce a new generation of Black teachers and other professionals.

This initiative was not without its critics. The right argued that Black access courses lowered admission standards and the left was concerned about tokenism and institutionalized marginalization. Some commentators also questioned whether such courses simply added another barrier to Black people's entry to higher education and professional careers as some of them led no further. The Commission for Racial Equality (CRE) argued that the concept of Black access did not address marginalization but instead sustained it – that it represented no more than 'a gesture of easily forgotten intent to ease any government conscience' (CRE, cited in White, 1985: 302). The gist of the CRE's opposition was that institutions should be recruiting Black people to mainstream courses and removing barriers to Black people's access to the power structures within the education system (Commission for Racial Equality, 1985).

The Manchester Black Access Course was different. For a start, it was linked with local polytechnics and colleges of higher education, which meant that students who were successful on the access programme had automatic entry to a place on a degree programme. Abasindi members were among the first people to enter higher education through this partnership. Another difference was that most of the teaching staff and management of the Manchester course were Black, and a third difference was that the course incorporated an overtly politicized approach within its taught components and included space for the exploration of Black studies alongside other subjects.

Across the educational and political establishment, there was little overall support for Black access courses, but at the time, the Manchester course achieved a reputation as 'one of the most effective models available' (White, 1985: 301). In an interview for this book, one of the Black women who taught on the Manchester Black Access Course from 1989 to 1996 and who was closely aligned with the Abasindi Cooperative reflects:

> The Manchester Black Access Course came into being after the 1981 uprising. At one level it was an initiative to get the community to police itself – since initially the programme was designed to prepare students for teacher training, social work or youth and community work. It was about progressing people who had been disadvantaged at school onto higher education. One of the admission exercises was to ask people to write about their educational experiences. The stories were amazing and although school hadn't always messed people up, students said they had not been encouraged; some were taken out of class to do sport, while others were told they wouldn't amount to anything. We were trying to address an imbalance. We had a foundation programme for people with no qualifications at all and an access programme for people with GCSEs. In fact the access year

was seen as part of the university degree structure and students were able to get a full grant for four or five years of study including the access part of it. Later, links were made with social sciences, history, psychology and English. Successful students were guaranteed a place at Manchester Polytechnic (now Manchester Metropolitan University); the university would interview the candidate as part of the access admission process and people were allocated places on one of the respective degree courses.

I wanted to encourage and empower our youth but needed to be realistic about a person's ability to manage a university degree. If teachers haven't taken the time to give you the tools you need then you will struggle to do the job. I saw the access course as a way of giving people tools. Our way of teaching was not just talk and chalk. Although we sometimes had formal lectures, most of our teaching was done through seminars and discussions, encouraging debate and critical thinking. Our teaching team was interdisciplinary and our curriculum political. We were very much influenced by the South African struggles and Pan-Africanism, and we wanted to raise political consciousness among the students, empowering them to question everything that was taken for granted.

Alongside other subjects like English, maths and the social sciences, we incorporated cultural studies, and we integrated African history into almost all our teaching. We explored history from an Africanist perspective and examined pre-slavery, slavery, colonialism and post-colonial periods. I was inspired by Ngugi's call for the decolonization of the mind. The students blossomed intellectually and questioned deeply, and our progression rate was very high. I remember one young woman who had come on the course because she wanted to do something for her kids saying 'this is the best educational experience I have ever had'. To see her grow through the programme was amazing – she moved on to complete her master's. The course helped people to find a voice and they were then able to act on that voice – one, for instance, went on to local politics. The students were mainly Black British of African and Caribbean descent; there were some Asian students and at one time the group included an Iranian. In the seven years that I taught on the course, the students were predominantly women.

Although most of the feedback was positive, there was one student who had grown up in foster care, in a White environment, for whom the course had a major emotional impact and she left the course. Society can be really damaging to Black people's identities and this opened a can of worms for me. I really wondered whether we knew what we were doing when it came to identity issues; I think there was probably a need to build in more support for people who had had negative personal experiences.

As for how many students made it through to completion of their degrees, I don't know. From the start there were constant attempts to dismantle the programme and nothing is documented about our successes. From the outside there was a lot of negativity towards the course. We had to fight to defend it; the major discourse around was that it was rubbish, a 'Mickey Mouse' course where people just sat around and chatted. Personally I didn't need to defend it, I kept seeing people do incredibly well – this spoke for itself. One important testimony was seeing one of our past students become a university lecturer. And when it came up for revalidation there were no criticisms of the course except that our assessment requirements were too high.

Some students inevitably didn't make it to the completion of their degrees, in some instances they had progressed before they were ready, and I don't mean academically: some students couldn't bridge the gap between intellectual ability and translating ideas on to paper, and some students withdrew or failed their university courses. But my recollection is that most of the students did well. Now, when you try to find anything out, all the information about the numbers of Black students we helped is gone, wiped away, like we never existed.

The course was dismantled in the 1990s with education reforms and changes to the Section 11 funding (Race Relations Act) that had provided much of the financial support. And as for now, so many kids are going to fail and fall out of the system, I can see that we will need a type of Black access course again in the future. This time, though, the focus should not be on finding a voice but on giving a counter voice that interrupts all the negative stuff going on right now with our children. It bothers me about the sexual objectification of girls, how

> boys are treating them and how girls exploit their own bodies, and it bothers me that when it comes to education, Black children are still being put into boxes and written off.
>
> (Anonymous)

The Manchester Black Access Course illustrates a political agenda aimed at challenging social injustice in education. After the 1981 disturbances, several Labour-controlled local education authorities (LEAs) established initiatives such as this, partly to address the inequalities that provoked the uprisings and also to challenge the New Right policies of the Thatcher government (Weiner, 1997). The concern expressed by the Commission for Racial Equality in 1985 about the marginalizing effect of Black access courses was to prove prophetic, since the education reforms of the late 1980s and 1990s curtailed the powers of LEAs and led to a withdrawal of funding. This caused the demise of equality education programmes that were not part of the mainstream of education provision. Nevertheless the success of the Black access courses in FE colleges, alongside other equality initiatives such as community education programmes and literacy campaigns, led to a noticeable rise in the number of Black students of African, Asian and Caribbean descent entering further and higher education institutions, from 8.5 per cent in 1991/2 to 9.8 per cent in 1993/4 (Avari *et al.*, 1997). As for Abasindi, the organization benefited greatly. Not only did we have a positive education programme to channel the talent and ambition of the women we worked with, but those of us who had been involved with the course were strengthened personally, professionally and politically.

Chapter 8

Reflections

As Black women, both academics working in higher education institutions, one with a background in youth and community work and the other in social work, the trials of institutional racism and gender discrimination are written large upon our histories. At the personal level, it is not being Black or being female that creates the challenges we face, but being at the nexus of race and gender. In the academic setting, although gender clearly matters and has mattered to us at every level of our progression, the injustices we encounter seem mostly to have their roots in racism. This is borne out by evidence discussed in Chapter 7 that shows that while women represent 44 per cent of academics in UK universities, the proportion of Black academics remains disproportionately low at 1.6 per cent.

Our immersion in the Abasindi Black Women's Cooperative at a time when our careers were just beginning, emboldened us to stand tall when we were expected to sit, to speak up in engulfing silence and to throw a spanner in the works when acquiescence with injustice was called for. Though we've been enraged at the discrimination we have witnessed, rage is a difficult emotion to sustain and there came a time when it seemed more sensible and more potent to write the words down than to speak them out. Beyond the academic mandate 'publish or perish', writing has therefore become something of a passion of politics for us both – a crucial strategy for the social activist. But ours is not a calcified approach that assumes cognitive knowledge to be enough and we have been preoccupied equally with the knowledge of our experience, of emotion and of the relevance and application of our writings for human rights.

Separately, we have researched and written about many different kinds of injustice: gender-based violence, immigration controls, child abuse, Black children in care, racial and gender inequalities. And we have written to advance our professional disciplines: social work and youth and community work. Accustomed to the unease caused by our constant clamour against inequality, those around us might have wondered whether we had become quieter. We had not; we had simply become smarter. Replacing the placard with the pen is a political act in itself and documenting the achievements and challenges of Abasindi seemed to us to be one of the most important contributions to Black struggle we could make. This is the first time we have

Reflections

written jointly but so seamless was the process that, together with the other women who contributed to the book, we became but a single historian drawing on multiple perspectives.

The African proverb states: 'Until the lions have their own historians, the history of the hunt will always glorify the hunter'. In retelling Abasindi's story through the perspectives of its women, the hunter is revealed: the successes were not all his; the lion was strategic, stealthy and brave – but for the hunter's dependence on his weapons of destruction the ending would have been quite different – a shallow victory indeed.

The book contains valuable information for students and academics in the fields of sociology, gender and race studies but we hope it will also help to inspire the activists of the future. We conclude by highlighting some of the most valuable lessons that have inspired our own activism.

Self-representation

Abasindi women believed that reclaiming representations of Blackness contained the potential to unsettle universalisms about dominant prescriptions of beauty that constrain all women – but also to confront racist ideologies within which these prescriptions are embedded and that constrain the freedom of Black women in particular.

For the Black woman, then, it is not only the fields, the workplace, the family or the institutions that are the site of her struggles but also her skin, her body and her hair. The celebration of skin, body and hair that surfaced within the context of the Abasindi Cooperative suggested an act of insurgency, whether conscious or not. The championing of hair left natural and the perfecting of African hairstyles, the love of Black skin rather than its grading by shade, and the assertion that the Black woman's body, however shaped, is unto itself beautiful but that, more than this, it is hers and hers alone, reveals a reclamation of self

Reclaiming representations of Blackness (Afua)

that is the starting point for political activism. Within a context in which beauty is highly commoditized and driven by ethnocentric aesthetic values, the choices a Black woman makes about how to represent her identity, style, desires and realities often carry meanings deep below the surface. A lesson indelibly etched on us by being part of Abasindi was the recognition that a female body that is undisciplinable rather than constrained is more than mere symbol of freedom, it is freedom itself. As the images that are woven throughout this book reveal, we fashioned ourselves in our own likeness and what emerged were diverse, multiple representations of the Black woman – traditional, contemporary, natural and straightened – we wore them all.

Self-expression

In her Nobel Prize lecture, Toni Morrison argued that language constitutes political action in itself and is not just product or artefact. One of the authors of this book once asked her Sierra Leonean father why he had never taught her any African languages. He replied that as a child growing up in Freetown, he had been beaten if he spoke anything other than 'proper' English – his own African language was quite literally whipped out of him. He recalled being made to recite Victorian poetry at the age of 5 to aged aunts on Sunday afternoons so as to perfect his enunciation.

Sierra Leone has long reclaimed its indigenous languages and the descendants of freed slaves who mainly live in the country's capital and who account for less than 6 per cent of the total population, have elevated their language of Krio (an English-based Creole), crafted out of that discomfiting history, to such a status that it is spoken by almost everyone in the country. It is the medium of instruction in many schools, the primary language of television and radio broadcasts, and political speeches are often delivered in Krio. One of the earliest post-independence acts of reclamation of language as a political act was the translation of some of Shakespeare's plays into Krio – we think Toni Morrison would nod in appreciation. Films have been made in Krio, academic books written, the Universal Declaration of Human Rights has been translated into Krio, and so has the Bible. Within Sierra Leone it now seems a mere irrelevance that the official language of the country is English, a matter more of international expediency than regard for an imposed mother tongue. Language is about consensus, the vernacular that flowers in specific contexts is simply the agreed medium for the transmission of linguistic signifiers and meanings; in Sierra Leone, the people speak Krio and Krio speaks for the people.

Understanding the historical significance of language and the ways in which language can be used as a tool of liberation was an important lesson from the Abasindi Cooperative. Poets SuAndi and Shirley May, whose poems feature in this book, flex their creative muscles against the constraints of formal English to write in ways that speak *for* and *to* Black people. This is not simply poetic licence; these poets are fierce defenders of race and gender equality and their choice of language stands as an opposition to systems of hegemony.

The late Victoria McKenzie, a poet, storyteller and author, and one of Abasindi's iconic figures, described her proudest achievement: the book she produced in Jamaican Patois. Vicky had become aware that children who spoke Patois were disadvantaged in British schools and she worked to undo the misapprehension that Patois characterized its speakers as unintelligent or uneducated. She had learned this from first-hand experience; Vicky had been one of the workers recruited from Jamaica in the 1950s and 1960s to shore up the labour needs of the mother country. But it was only her labour that was wanted, not her career aspirations or her gifts as an artist, and she found it impossible to gain access to higher education or to obtain work in the arts. Her Jamaican accent and Patois were the auditory equivalent of the symbol of intellectual inferiority that was attached to being Black. Vicky spoke of the obstacles she had faced and her frustrations over being unable to fulfil her potential. She was determined that subsequent generations would have the opportunities that had been denied her. Her mission was to get Patois recognized as a language in its own right, not an inferior form of English or simply the language of the streets. As she said, 'it's a language that empowers its speakers and gives them the right to their own cultural, social and political identity'. Vicky saw all of this in the Jamaican Patois of her homeland, a message she spread among schools and community organizations within Moss Side. Krio, poetry, storytelling and Patois are all forms of self-expression but when reclaimed as a political act, they are also a means of challenging the racial hierarchies of language.

Self-learning

Within the Black community, success is often linked to educational achievements. Within Moss Side, parental influence, community education projects and cultural activities were among the key factors believed to contribute to the academic success of African-Caribbean children in the UK. However, the thwarting of academic progress through the systemic and institutionalized underdevelopment of Black children's abilities has been a long-standing battle for parents. Abasindi, like many other Black organizations in the 1970s and 1980s, set up a free Saturday Supplementary

School to support children of Moss Side to gain the educational skills they needed for success.

Scholars have differentiated between the male strategies of securing social resources and the female strategies of constructing social capital as two versions of community activism – 'his and hers'. Abasindi Saturday School was built on the 'hers' model: it was mainly women who were responsible for its organization even though both male and female university students volunteered as tutors. In addition to the provision of supplementary teaching, especially in the areas of mathematicss and English, the programme also focused on 'tools to survive racism' in recognition of the fact that in this society, specific attention is needed to help Black children develop a positive sense of identity, pride and belonging. Many of the Abasindi women did not feel fully at home in Britain, even if born in the UK. One's status as outsider was inferred by skin colour alone and constantly reinforced at both the discursive level and within one's daily reality. 'Where are you from?' was an explicit question that preceded many conversations and, buried behind this, the implicit question, 'why are you here?' demanded justification for our presence. This is not the case for our children and grandchildren; they do not carry the burden of justifying their existence in the UK – this is as much their land as anyone's. Louise Da-Cocodia, who worked alongside Abasindi, stated that the aim of her community work was to 'help young Black people understand that this is their home, this is the society they live in, and that they have a part to play in developing it'.

However, the growing far-right groups in the UK and the persistence of racist ideologies continue to threaten the right of Black people to live freely and safely within the UK's borders, especially the young. The racist murder of Stephen Lawrence stands as a key marker of this awful reality. Stephen was murdered in 1993, simply because he was Black. The tireless campaign of his parents, particularly his mother Doreen, resulted in two of his killers being imprisoned (three remain at large), and uncovered the extent of racism and the complicity of some police officers in London. Her campaign against racial injustice has earned her many accolades: she was appointed to the House of Lords as a Labour Peer in 2013 and was named by Radio 4's *Woman's Hour* as the country's leading 'game changer' of 2014, an award celebrating women who changed the face of power in the UK. In establishing the Stephen Lawrence Charitable Trust in 1993, Stephen's parents' aims were to support young people to achieve their education and career aspirations. This message resonates with the lessons of the Abasindi Cooperative: Black children belong in the UK and we must continue to fight to ensure they have the same access to opportunity as anyone else. Education cannot, of itself, prevent our children being exposed to racist attacks, inequality or injustice but their achievements signal a refusal to be constrained by racism, and stand as testament to the resilience Abasindi engendered.

'The children are the flowers of our struggle and the principal reason for our fight.' (Amilcar Cabral, 1975)

From left to right, top: Zinzi, Nkosi, Dziko; bottom: Abubakarr, Yinka, Thembi

References

Abdul-Raheem, T. (ed.) (1996) *Pan Africanism: Politics, economy and social change in the twenty-first century*. London: Pluto Press.

Adair, C. and Burt, R. (2013) *British Dance Black Routes*. Online. http://dancehe.org.uk/wp-content/uploads/2014/03/British-Dance-Black-Routes.pdf (accessed 21 May 2015).

Adichie, C.N. (2013) *Americanah: A Novel*. New York: Knopf.

Afrika Global Network (n.d.) 'Special Documents'. Online. www.afrikaglobalnetwork.com/htm/leopold.htm (accessed 14 June 2015).

Alexander, H. (2013) 'Nelson Mandela, Madiba, Tata – What's in a name?' *The Telegraph*, 6 December. Online. www.telegraph.co.uk/news/worldnews/nelson-mandela/10501587/Nelson-Mandela-Madiba-Tata-whats-in-a-name.html (accessed 1 June 2015).

Alexander, Z. and Dewjee, A. (eds) (1984) *The Wonderful Adventures of Mrs Seacole in Many Lands*. Bristol: Falling Wall Press.

Alleyne, M.C. (1988) *Roots of Jamaican Culture*. London: Pluto Press.

Andersen, M. and Collins, P.H. (eds) (2001) *Race, Class and Gender: An anthology*. 4th ed. Belmont, CA: Wadsworth.

Andrews, K. (2013) *Resisting Racism: Race, inequality, and the Black supplementary school movement*. London: Trentham Books.

Anonymous (2003) 'Letter to a social worker: Reflections on mothering'. In Douglas, A. and Philpot, T. (eds) *Adoption: Changing families, changing times*. London: Routledge, 91–8.

Ashe, F. (2014) 'All about Eve: Mothers, masculinities and the 2011 UK riots'. *Political Studies*, 62 (3), 652–68.

Association of Dance of the African Diaspora (2013a) 'Book review: *Dancing the Black Question: The Phoenix Dance Company Phenomenon*'. Online. www.adad.org.uk/metadot/index.pl?id=24393&isa=Category (accessed 10 June 2015).

Association of Dance of the African Diaspora (2013b) 'Training – study, experiences and results'. Online. www.adad.org.uk/metadot/index.pl?id=22805&isa=Category&op=show (accessed 10 June 2015).

Avari, B., Jones, H.M.F., Mashengele, D. and Patel, K. (1997) '"Race" and "Ethnicity"'. In *Crossing Borders, Breaking Boundaries: Research in the education of adults*. Proceedings of the 27th Annual SCUTREA Conference. *Adult Education: Issues of power and diversity*.

Baker, H. (2009) '"Potentially violent men?" Teenage boys, access to refuges and constructions of men, masculinity and violence'. *Journal of Social Welfare and Family Law*, 31 (4), 435–50.

Banner, R. (2013) 'Surface and stasis: Re-reading slave narrative via *The History of Mary Prince*'. *Callaloo*, 36 (2), 298–311, 505.

Barker, G.T. (2005) *Dying to be Men: Youth, masculinity and social exclusion*. London: Routledge.

References

Barn, R. (2000) 'Race, ethnicity and transracial adoption'. In Katz, I. and Treacher, A. (eds) *The Dynamics of Adoption*. London: Jessica Kingsley Publishers, 111–26.

Barn, R. and Kirton, D. (2012) 'Transracial adoption in Britain: Politics, ideology and reality'. *Adoption & Fostering*, 36 (3–4), 25–37.

Barrett, L.B. (1976) *The Sun and the Drum: African roots in Jamaican folk tradition*. Kingston and London: Heinemann.

BBC News (1982) 'UK unemployment tops three million'. Online. http://news.bbc.co.uk/onthisday/hi/dates/stories/january/26/newsid_2506000/2506335.stm (accessed 22 May 2015).

Beckford, G.L. and Levitt, K. (2000) *The George Beckford Papers*. Jamaica: Canoe Press.

Beckles, H.M. (1989) *Natural Rebels: A social history of enslaved Black women in Barbados*. New York: Rutgers University Press.

— (2002) 'Crop over fetes and festivals in Caribbean slavery'. In Thompson, A.O. (ed.) *In the Shadow of the Plantation: Carribbean history and legacy*. Kingston: Ian Randle, 246–65.

Belton, B.A. (2007) *Black Routes: Legacy of African Diaspora*. London and Hertfordshire: Hansib Publications UK.

Bennett, L. (1966) *Jamaican Labrish*. Jamaica: Sangsters Book Stores.

Bennett, O. (1987) *The Nia Cultural Centre: A feasibility study on the housing and management of a Black cultural centre in the BBC Playhouse, Hulme, Manchester, Part One: Consultant's report*.

Best, S. and Marcus, S. (2009) 'Surface reading: An introduction'. *Representations*, 108 (1), 1–21.

Bhabha, J. and Shutter, S. (1994) *Women's Movement: Women under immigration, nationality and refugee law*. London: Trentham Books.

Blackburn, F. (2005) 'Developing Black identity'. In Healicon, A. and Sapin, K. (eds) *A Black Perspective in Community and Youth Work: A Community Work Unit Conference*, University of Manchester. Online. www.escholar.manchester.ac.uk/api/datastream?publicationPid=uk-ac-man-scw:198513&datastreamId=FULL-TEXT.PDF (accessed 22 May 2015).

Blair, S. (2007) *Harlem Crossroads: Black writers and the photograph in the twentieth century*. Princeton, NJ: Princeton University Press.

Bourdieu, P. and Passeron, J-C. (1977) *Reproduction in Education, Society and Culture*. Trans. Nice, R. London and Beverly Hills: Sage.

Brah, A. (1991) 'Difference, diversity, differentiation'. *International Review of Sociology*, 2 (2), 53–71.

Bridges, L. (2012) 'Four days in August: The UK riots'. *Race & Class*, 54 (1), 1–12.

Brown, B. (2014) 'More Than Just Hair Talk: The kinks, curls and dueling feminisms in YouTube's natural hair community'. MA thesis, The Pennsylvania State University, The Graduate School College of Communications. Online. https://etda.libraries.psu.edu/paper/21239/22037 (accessed 12 July 2014).

Bryan, B., Dadzie, S. and Scafe, S. (1985) *The Heart of the Race: Black women's lives in Britain*. London: Virago.

Burman, E., Smailes, S.L. and Chantler, K. (2004) 'Culture as a barrier to service provision and delivery: Domestic violence services for minoritized women'. *Critical Social Policy*, 24 (3), 332–57.

Campbell, B. (1993) *Goliath: Britain's dangerous places*. London: Methuen.
Campbell, G. (1990) 'History makers'. In Davies, C.B. and Fido, E.S. (eds) *Out of the Kumbla: Caribbean women and literature*. Trenton, NJ: Africa World Press.
Carlton-LaNey, I.B. (2001) *African American Leadership: An empowerment tradition in social welfare history*. Washington, DC: NASW Press.
Carter, T. (1986) *Shattering Illusions: West Indians in British politics*. London: Lawrence & Wishart.
Chakrabarti, M. and Hill, M. (2000) *Residential Child Care: International perspectives on links with families and peers*. London: Jessica Kingsley.
Cheng, A.A. (2000) 'Wounded beauty: An exploratory essay on race, feminism, and the aesthetic question'. *Tulsa Studies in Women's Literature*, 19 (2), 191–217. Online. www.jstor.org/stable/464426 (accessed 11 June 2014).
Chevannes, M. and Reeves, F. (1987) 'The Black voluntary school movement: Definition, contexts and prospects'. In Troyna, B. (ed.) *Racial Inequality in Education*. London: Tavistock, 147–69.
Clark, K.B. and Clark, M.K. (1939) 'The development of consciousness of self and the emergence of racial identification in Negro preschool children'. *Journal of Social Psychology*, 10 (4), 591–9.
— (1947) 'Racial identification and preference in Negro children'. In Newcomb, T.M. and Hartley, E.L. (eds) *Readings in Social Psychology*. New York: Holt, Rinehart & Winston.
Clarke, J. (2003) 'Celebrating struggle: A reflection of Black women's stories – The South African Truth and Reconciliation Commission: Conference Report'.
Coard, B. (1971) *How the West Indian Child is Made Educationally Sub-normal in the British School System: The scandal of the black child in schools in Britain*. London: New Beacon.
Cobham, R. (1990) 'Women in Jamaican literature 1900–1950'. In Davies, C.B. and Fido, E.S. (eds) *Out of the Kumbla*. Trenton, NJ: Africa World Press, 195–221.
Cohen, S. (2006) *Standing on the Shoulders of Fascism: From immigration control to the strong state*. Stoke-on-Trent: Trentham Books.
Collins, M. (1988) 'Women writers from the Caribbean'. *Spare Rib*, 94, 20.
Collins, P.H. (1990) *Black Feminist Thought: Knowledge, consciousness and the politics of empowerment*. New York and Boston: Unwin Hyman.
— (1998) 'The tie that binds: Race, gender and US violence'. *Ethnic and Racial Studies*, 21 (5), 917–38.
Collins, S. (1957) *Coloured Minorities in Britain: Studies in British race relations based on African, West Indian and Asiatic immigrants*. London: Lutterworth Press.
Commission for Racial Equality (1985) *Swann: A Response from the Commission for Racial Equality*. London: Commission for Racial Equality.
Connell, R.W. and Messerschmidt, J.W. (2005) 'Hegemonic masculinities: Rethinking the concept'. *Gender and Society*, 19 (6), 829–59.
Cross, M. (n.d.) 'Black unemployment and racial conflict'. Evidence submitted to the Scarman Tribunal. Unpublished. Available from Research Unit on Ethnic Relations, St Peter's College, Saltley, Birmingham B8 3TE.
Cross, W.E. (1971) 'The Negro to Black conversion experience: Toward a psychology of Black liberation'. *Black World*, 20 (9), 13–27.

References

Dalphinis, M. (1978) *Approaches to the Study of Creole Languages: The case for West African language influences*. London: Black Liberator.

Dargie, D. (1992) *Musical Practices of the Xhosa People*. Cape Town: David Phillips.

Davey, A. (1983) *Learning to be Prejudiced: Growing up in multi-ethnic Britain*. London: Edward Arnold.

Davies, C.B and Ogundipe-Leslie, M. (1995) *Moving Beyond Boundaries, Vol 1: International Dimensions of Black Women's Writing*. New York: New York University Press.

Davis, A.Y. (1981) *Women, Race and Class*. New York: Random House.

Davis, E., Watt, D. and Packham, C. (2012) *Aspiration and Engagement: Strategies for working with young Black men*. Manchester: MMU Community Audit and Evaluation Centre.

Daycare Trust (2011) *Childcare Sufficiency Assessment: Moss Side ward report: Central West District*. London: Daycare Trust. Online. www.manchester.gov.uk/download/downloads/id/.../moss_side_ward (accessed 10 June 2015).

Day, T. (1994) 'Sisters under the Skin', *Education Guardian*, 27 September.

Deck, A. (1996) 'Review: *The History of Mary Prince, a West Indian Slave, Related by Herself*'. *African American Review*, 30 (2), 297–9.

Douglas, J.D. (1985) *Caribbean Man's Blues*. London: Akira Press.

Dove, N. (1998) *African Mothers*. New York: State University of New York Press.

Dumper, H. (2005) *Refugee Council: Making women visible: Strategies for a more woman-centred asylum and refugee support system*. London: Refugee Council.

Edwards-Kerr, D. (2005) 'Understanding the Educational Needs of African-Caribbean Young Men and Developing Pathways for Action'. PhD diss., Manchester University.

Ekejuiba, A.F. (1995) 'Gender-responsive agenda for equitable development'. In Pala, A.O. (ed.) *Connecting Across Cultures and Continents: Black women speak out on identity, race, and development*. New York: United Nations Development Fund for Women, 53–72.

Euba, A. (1992) 'Yoruba music in the Church: The development of a neo-African art among the Yoruba of Nigeria'. In DjeDje, J.C. (ed.) *African Musicology: Current trends: Volume two. A festschrift presented to J.H. Kwabena Nketia*. Atlanta, GA: Crossroads Press, 45–63.

Fanon, F. (1968) *The Wretched of the Earth*. New York: Grove Press.

Farrar, M. (1989) 'Better Mus' Come': Rethinking community as a radical social imaginary'. Unpublished essay, Leeds University.

Fitzpatrick, L.A. (2012) 'African Names and Naming Practices: The impact slavery and European domination had on the African psyche, identity and protest'. MA thesis, Ohio State University. Online. http://afrikannames.com/wp-content/uploads/2013/06/Fitzpatrick-Liseli-A.pdf (accessed 10 June 2015).

Flaig, V.H. (2010) 'The Politics of Representation and Transmission in the Globalization of Guinea's Djembé'. PhD diss., University of Michigan. Online. http://deepblue.lib.umich.edu/bitstream/handle/2027.42/75801/vhflaig_1.pdf?sequence=1&isAllowed=y (accessed 10 December 2014).

Folami O.M. (2013) 'Survey of unreported cases of domestic violence in two heterogeneous communities in Nigeria'. *International Review of Law*. Online. dv.4 http://dx.doi.org/ 10.5339/irl.2013.dv.4 (accessed 14 June 2015).

Fook, J. and Askeland, G.A. (2007) 'Challenges of critical reflection: "Nothing ventured, nothing gained"'. *Social Work Education*, 26 (5), 520–33.

Ford-Smith, H. (1988) 'Women and the Garvey movement in Jamaica'. In Lewis, R. and Bryan, P.E. (eds) *Garvey: His work and impact*. Kingston, Mona: ISER and UWI Extra Mural Studies Department.

Frost, D. and Phillips, R. (eds) (2011) *Liverpool '81: Remembering the riots*. Liverpool: Liverpool University Press.

Fryer, P. (1984) *Staying Power: The history of Black people in Britain*. London and Sydney: Pluto Press.

Gabriel, D. (2013) 'Race equality in academia: Time to establish black studies in the UK?' *The Guardian*, 25 July. Online. www.theguardian.com/higher-education-network/blog/2013/jul/25/race-equality-academia-curriculum (accessed 22 May 2015).

Gilchrist, E.S. and Thompson, C. (2012) 'African-American women's perceptions of constitutive meanings of good hair articulated in Black hair magazine advertisements'. *Journalism and Mass Communication*, 2 (1), 279–93.

Gillborn, D. (2004) 'Racism, policy and contemporary schooling: Current inequities and future possibilities'. *Sage Race Relations Abstracts*, 29 (2), 5–33.

Gilroy, P. (1987) *There Ain't No Black in the Union Jack: The cultural politics of race and nation*. London: Hutchinson.

Glass, R. and Pollins, H. (1960) *Newcomers: The West Indians in London*. London: University College London Centre for Urban Studies, and Allen and Unwin.

Glendinning, A. (2011) 'Moss Side riots: Doctor who had to help despite the risks'. *Manchester Evening News*, 6 July. Online. http://menmedia.co.uk/manchestereveningnews/news/s/1425816_moss-side-riots-doctor-who-had-to-help-despite-the-risks (accessed 22 May 2015).

Gower, M. (2013) *Ending Child Immigration Detention*. London: House of Commons Library.

Graham, M. and Robinson, G. (2004) '"The silent catastrophe": Institutional racism in the British educational system and the underachievement of black boys'. *Journal of Black Studies*, 34 (5), 653–71.

Gramsci, A., and Hoare, Q. (1978) *Selections from Political Writings (1921–1926): With additional texts by other Italian communist leaders*. London: Lawrence and Wishart.

The Guardian/London School of Economics (2011) 'Reading the riots: Investigating England's summer of disorder'. Online. www.guardian.co.uk/uk/interactive/2011/dec/14/reading-the-riots-investigating-england-s-summer-of-disorder-full-report (accessed 30 September 2014).

Haraway, D.J. (1989) *Primate Visions: Gender, Race, and Nature in the World of Modern Science*. London: Routledge.

— (1992) 'Ecce homo, ain't (ar'n't) I a woman, and inappropriate/d others: The human in a post-humanist landscape'. In Butler, J. and Scott, J.W. (eds) *Feminists Theorize the Political*. London: Routledge, 86–100.

Harker, R. and Heath, S. (2012) *Children in Care in England: Statistics*. Online. www.parliament.uk/briefing-papers/sn04470.pdf (accessed 20 July 2014).

Henriques, F. (1960) *Jamaica, Land of Wood and Water*. New York: MacGibbon & Kee.

References

Hey, V. (1998) 'Reading the community: A critique of some post/modern narratives about citizenship and civil society'. In Baguley, P. and Hearn, G. (eds) *Transforming the Political*. London: Macmillan.

Hick, P. (2010) *Manchester Conference for Black Parents, Children and Young People: Public Engagement Fellowship Conference Report*. Manchester: Manchester Metropolitan University, Louise Da-Cocodia Education Trust.

Hick, P., Arshad, R., Mitchell, L., Watt, D. and Roberts. L. (2011) *Promoting Cohesion, Challenging Expectations: Educating the teachers of tomorrow for race equality and diversity in 21st century schools*. Manchester: Manchester Metropolitan University, CERES.

Higher Education Statistics Agency (n.d.) 'Free online statistics: Staff'. Online. www.hesa.ac.uk/index.php?option=com_content&view=article&id=1898 (accessed 10 June 2015).

Hill, R.B. (2003) *The Strengths of Black Families*. Lanham, MD: University Press of America.

Hill Collins, P. (1998) 'Intersections of race, class, gender, and nation: Some implications for black family studies'. *Journal of Comparative Family Studies*, 29 (1), 27–34.

Hinds, D. (2008) Claudia Jones and the 'West Indian Gazette'. Online. www.irr.org.uk/news/claudia-jones-and-the-west-indian-gazette (accessed 29 December 2014)

Holmes, R. (2007) *African Queen: The real life of the Hottentot Venus*. New York: Random House.

hooks, b. (1994) *Outlaw Culture: Resisting representations*. London: Routledge.

— (1997) *Killing Rage, Ending Racism*. New York: Holt Paperbacks.

— (2003) *Teaching Community: A pedagogy of hope*. New York: Routledge.

Hytner, B. (1981) *Report of the Moss Side Enquiry to the Leader of the GMC*. Manchester: Greater Manchester Council.

Impey, A. (1998) 'Popular music in Africa'. In Stone, R. (ed.) *The Garland Encyclopedia of World Music*. New York: Garland Publishing, 87–8.

International Rescue Committee (2012) *Let Me Not Die Before My Time: Domestic violence in West Africa*. New York: IRC.

Irie Dance Theatre (2014) Online. www.iriedancetheatre.org/#sthash.GGlEb8uw.dpuf (accessed 8 June 2015).

Jackson, R.L. (2006) *Scripting the Black Masculine Body: Identity, discourse, and racial politics in popular media*. Albany, NY: State University of New York Press.

Jacques Garvey, A. (1972) 'The role of women in liberation struggles'. *The Massachusetts Review*, 13 (1–2), 109–12.

Jarrett-Macauley, D. (1998) *The Life of Una Marson, 1905–65*. Manchester: Manchester University Press.

Javed, H.M. (2012) 'What does it mean to move from magical consciousness to critical consciousness?' Unpublished diss., Manchester Metropolitan University.

John, G. (2006) *Taking a Stand: Gus John speaks on education, race, social action & civil unrest 1980–2005*. Manchester: Gus John Partnership.

Jones, A. and Waul, D. (2005) 'Residential care for Black children'. In Crimmens, D. and Milligan, I. (eds) *Facing Forward: Residential care in the 21st century*. London: Russell House Publishing, 31–44.

Jones, A.D. and Jemmott, E.T. (2014). 'Status, privilege and gender inequality: Cultures of male impunity and entitlement in the sexual abuse of children: Perspectives from a Caribbean study'. *International Social Work*. Online. http://isw.sagepub.com/content/early/2014/09/05/0020872814537853.full.pdf+html(accessed 22 May 2015, requires subscription).

Kankpeyeng, B.W. (2009) 'The Slave Trade in Northern Ghana: Landmarks, legacies and connections'. *Slavery & Abolition*, 30 (2), 209–221.

Karn, V. (1983) 'Race and housing in Britain: The role of major institutions'. In Glazer, N. and Young, K. (eds) *Ethnic Pluralism and Public Policy: Achieving equality in the United States and Britain*. London: Heinemann, 162–83.

King, D.K. (1988) 'Multiple jeopardy, multiple consciousness: The context of a Black feminist ideology'. *Signs*, 14 (1), 42–72.

Kirwen, M.C. (2008) *African Cultural Domains, Book 1*. Nairobi: MIAS Books.

Kruczkowska, F.M. (2007) 'Book Review: "Dancing the Black Question: The Phoenix Dance Company Phenomenon"'. *Association of Dance of the African Diaspora*. Online. www.adad.org.uk/metadot/index.pl?iid=24393 (accessed 12 August 2015).

Kundnani, A. (2007a) *Echoes of Empire: Racism, migration and the war on terror*. London: Pluto Press.

— (2007b) *The End of Tolerance: Racism in 21st century Britain*. London: Pluto Press.

Larrabee, M.J. (2006) '"I know what a slave knows": Mary Prince's epistemology of resistance'. *Women's Studies: An inter-disciplinary journal*, 35 (5), 453–73.

La Rose, J., John, G. and Johnson, L.K. (2011) *The New Cross Massacre Story: Interviews with John La Rose*. London: New Beacon Books.

Lawrence, D. (1974) *Black Migrants: White Natives: A study of race relations in Nottingham*. Cambridge: Cambridge University Press.

Lea, J. and Hallsworth, S. (2012) 'Understanding the riots'. *Criminal Justice Matters*, 87 (1), 30–1.

Lea, J. and Young, J. (1982) 'The riots in Britain 1981: Urban violence and political marginalisation'. In Cowell, D., Jones, D. and Young, J. (eds) *Policing the Riots*. London: Junction Books, 5–20.

Lee, J. (2013) 'Why Nelson Mandela is called Madiba'. *Detroit Free Press*, 6 December. Online. http://archive.freep.com/article/20131206/NEWS15/312060072/Why-Nelson-Mandela-is-called-Madiba (accessed 1 June 2015).

Lee, J.A.B. (2001) *The Empowerment Approach to Social Work Practice: Building the beloved community*. 2nd ed. New York, Chichester: Columbia University Press.

Lewis, G (1993) 'Black women's employment and the British economy'. In James, W. and Harris, C. (eds) *Inside Babylon: The Caribbean Diaspora in Britain*. London: Verso, 73–96.

— (1996) 'Situated voices: Black women's experience and social work'. *Feminist Review*, 53 (1), 24–64.

Li, S. (2006) 'Motherhood as resistance in Harriet Jacobs's *Incidents in the Life of a Slave Girl*'. *Legacy*, 23 (1), 14–29.

Lorde, A. (1984) *Sister Outsider: Essays and speeches*. Berkeley, CA: Crossing Press.

— (1995) *The Black Unicorn: Poems*. New York: Norton and Company.

Lovejoy, P. (2007) Review: 'Rachel Holmes. *African Queen: The real life of the Hottentot Venus*'. *Journal of Historical Biography*, 2, 97–9. Online. www.ufv.ca/jhb/Volume_2/Volume_2_Lovejoy.pdf (accessed 22 May 2015).

Loveys, K. (2011) 'School that banned 11-year-old boy for having "cornrow" hairstyle was "racist", High Court judge rules'. *Daily Mail*, 18 June. Online. www.dailymail.co.uk/news/article-2004693/School-banned-11-year-old-boy-having-cornrow-hairstyle-racist-High-Court-judge-rules.html#ixzz37qoJnJtJ (accessed 15 July 2014).

Maathai, W. (2007) *Unbowed: One woman's story*. London: Heinemann.

Majors, R. (2001) *Educating Our Black Children: New directions and radical approaches*. London: Routledge.

Manchester Evening News (2011) 'Moss Side riots: The night years of anger exploded in an orgy of violence'. 4 July. Online. www.manchestereveningnews.co.uk/news/greater-manchester-news/moss-side-riots-the-night-years-864536 (accessed 22 May 2015).

Mann, S.A. and Grimes, M.D. (2001) 'Common and contested ground: Marxism and race, gender and class analysis'. *Race, Gender & Class*, 8 (2), 3–22.

Marco, J.L. (2012) 'Hair Representations Among Black South African Women: Exploring identity and notions of beauty'. MA Diss., University of South Africa. Online. http://uir.unisa.ac.za/bitstream/handle/10500/9204/dissertation_marco_jl.pdf?sequence=, (accessed 25 June 2014).

Matthews, M.D. (1979) '"Our women and what they think": Amy Jacques Garvey and the Negro world'. *The Black Scholar: Journal of Black Studies and Research*, 10, 8–9.

Maxime, J. (1986) 'Some psychological models of black self concept'. In Ahmed, S., Cheetham, J. and Small, J. (eds) *Social Work with Children and their Families*. London: Batsford.

Mercer, K. (1994) *Welcome to the Jungle: New positions in Black cultural studies*. London: Routledge.

— (1999) 'Black hair/style politics'. In Owusu, K. (ed.) *Black British Culture & Society: A text reader*. London and New York: Routledge, 111–21.

Messerschmidt, J.W. (2000) *Nine Lives: Adolescent masculinities, the body, and violence*. Boulder, CO: Westview.

Milburn, K. (2012) 'The August riots, shock and the prohibition of thought'. *Capital & Class*, 36 (3). 401–9.

Minshall, P. (2000) '"To Play Mas": Towards 2000 – Models for multi-cultural arts education'. *Caribbean Quarterly*, 45 (2/3), 30–5.

Mirza, H. (2009) *Race, Gender and Educational Desire: Why black women succeed and fail*. London: Routledge.

Morokvasic, M. (1983) 'Women in migration: Beyond the reductionist outlook'. In Phizacklea, A. (ed.) *One Way Ticket: Migration and female labour*. London: Routledge and Kegan Paul, 13–31.

Morrison, T. (1994) *The Bluest Eye*. New York: Plume.

— (1999) *The Bluest Eye*. New York: Random House.

Muir, H. and Adegoke, Y (2011) 'Were the riots about race?' *The Guardian*, 8 December. Online. www.theguardian.com/uk/2011/dec/08/were-the-riots-about-race (accessed 13 August 2014).

National Commission on Culture (2006) 'The Dance Company of Ghana'. Online. www.ghanaculture.gov.gh/index1.php?linkid=331&page=2&sectionid=661 (accessed 10 June 2015).

National Union of Students (2010) *Race for Equality: A report on the experiences of Black students in further and higher education*. Online. www.nus.org.uk/PageFiles/12350/NUS_Race_for_Equality_web.pdf (accessed 26 October 2014).

Nettleford, R.M. and LaYacona, M. (1985) *Dance Jamaica: Cultural definition and artistic discovery: The National Dance Theatre Company of Jamaica, 1962–1983*. New York: Grove Press.

Newburn, T. (2012) '30 years after Brixton, what would Lord Scarman have made of the 2011 riots?' *The Guardian*, 1 July. Online. www.theguardian.com/uk/2012/jul/01/brixton-lord-scarman-2011-riots (accessed 2 November 2014).

Newburn, T., Lewis, P. and Metcalf, J. (2011) 'A new kind of riot? From Brixton 1981 to Tottenham 2011'. *The Guardian*, 9 December. Online. www.guardian.co.uk/uk/2011/dec/09/riots-1981-2011-differences (accessed 20 October 2013).

New York Times (1981) 'Reports of police abuse studied in Manchester'. 22 July. Online. www.nytimes.com/1981/07/22/world/reports-of-police-abuse-studied-in-manchester.html (accessed 22 May 2015).

Nixon, J. and Humphreys, C. (2010) 'Marshalling the Evidence: Using intersectionality in the domestic violence frame'. *Social Politics: International studies in gender, state & society*, 17 (2), 137–58.

Nnaemeka, O. (1997) *The Politics of (M)othering*. London and New York: Routledge.

Nyamnjoh, F.B., Durham, D. and Fokwang, J.D. (2002) 'The domestication of hair and modernised consciousness in Cameroon: A critique in the context of globalisation'. *Identity, Culture and Politics*, 3 (2), 98–124.

Obadina, T. (1997) Review: '*Pan Africanism: Politics, economy and social change in the twenty-first century*. Edited by Tajudeen Abdul-Raheem'. *Development in Practice*, 7 (3), 315–17.

Omalade, B. (1994) *The Rising Song of African-American Women*. New York and London: Routledge.

Owen, C. and Statham, J. (2009) *Disproportionality in Child Welfare: The prevalence of black and minority ethnic children within 'looked after' and 'children in need' populations and on child protection registers in England* (Research Report DCSF-RR124). London: Thomas Coram Research Unit Institute of Education, University of London. Online. http://dera.ioe.ac.uk/11152/1/DCSF-RR124.pdf (accessed 25 June 2014).

Palmer, G. and Kenway, P. (2007) *Poverty Rates among Ethnic Groups in Great Britain*. York: Joseph Rowntree Foundation. Online. www.jrf.org.uk/publications/poverty-rates-among-ethnic-groups-great-britain (accessed 10 November 2014).

Pan-African Development Education and Advocacy Programme (n.d.) 'The history of Pan Africanism'. Online. www.padeap.net/the-history-of-pan-africanism (accessed 13 May 2015).

Parham, T.A. (1989) 'Cycles of psychological nigrecense'. *The Counseling Pyschologist*, 17 (2), 187–226.

Parr, C. (2014) 'Race discrimination in universities still a problem, reports survey'. *Times Higher Education*, 6 April. Online. www.timeshighereducation.co.uk/news/race...in...a.../2012474.article (accessed 22 May 2015).

References

Patterson, S. (1965) *Dark Strangers: A study of West Indians in London.* London: Penguin.

Pedraza, S. (1991) 'Women and migration: The social consequences of gender'. *Annual Review of Sociology,* 17 (1), 303–25.

Petromaxtheatre (2006) 'Working class women and their struggle'. Online. http://petromaxtheatre.blogspot.co.uk/2006/08/working-class-womentheir-struggle.html (accessed 14 June 2015).

Phillips, J., Ray, K. and Barnes, H. (2007) *Social Cohesion in Diverse Communities.* York: Joseph Rowntree Foundation.

Phillips, M. and Phillips, T. (1998) *Windrush: The irresistible rise of multi-racial Britain.* London: HarperCollins.

Phillips, R. (1975) 'The Black masses and the political economy of Manchester – Introduction'. *The Black Liberator,* 3 (3), 290–300.

Phinney, J.S. (1990) 'Ethnic identity in adolescents: Review of research'. *Psychological Bulletin,* 108 (3), 499–514.

Pilkington, A. (2003) *Racial Disadvantage and Ethnic Diversity in Britain.* Basingstoke: Palgrave Macmillan.

Pilkington, E. (2014) 'Caribbean nations prepare demand for slavery reparations'. *The Guardian,* 9 March. Online. www.theguardian.com/world/2014/mar/09/caribbean-nations-demand-slavery-reparations (accessed 12 December 2014).

Platts-Fowler, D. (2013) '"Beyond the loot": Social disorder and urban unrest'. *The British Society of Criminology,* 13, 17–32. Online. http://britsoccrim.org/new/volume13/pbcc_2013_Platts-Fowler.pdf (accessed 22 May 2015).

Plowden Report (1967) *Children and their Primary School.* London: HMSO.

Politics.co.uk 'Unemployment'. Online. www.politics.co.uk/reference/unemployment (accessed 25 October 2014).

Pollard, T.F. (2011) *The Black British Boy: Expressions of masculine cultural identity.* New York and London: Routledge.

Prasad, R. (2011) 'English riots were "a sort of revenge" against the police'. *The Guardian,* 5 December.

Prince, M. (1831) *The History of Mary Prince, a West Indian Slave.* Online. www.gutenberg.org/ebooks/17851 (accessed 12 December 2014).

Pryce, K. (1979) *Endless Pressure: A study of West Indian life-styles in Bristol.* London: Penguin.

Qyason, A. (2014) 'What it is to be Winnie Mandela'. Online. http://africasacountry.com/what-is-it-to-be-winnie-mandela/ (accessed 22 May 2015).

Ramdhanie, B. (2005) 'African Dance in England: Spirituality and continuity'. PhD thesis, University of Warwick. Online. http://webcat.warwick.ac.uk/record=b2072944~S9 (accessed 10 December 2014).

REACH (2007) *An Independent Report to Government on Raising Aspiration and Attainment of Black Boys and Young Black Men.* London: Department for Communities and Local Government. Online. http://dera.ioe.ac.uk/7609/7/reach-report_Redacted.pdf (accessed 8 August 2014).

Rex, J. (1982) 'The 1981 urban riots in Britain'. *International Journal of Urban and Regional Research,* 6 (1), 99–113.

Rhamie, J. and Hallam, S. (2002) 'An investigation into African-Caribbean academic success in the UK'. *Race Ethnicity and Education,* 5 (2), 151–70.

Richie, B.E. (2000) 'A Black feminist reflection on the antiviolence movement'. *Signs*, 25 (4), 1133–7.

Riley, D.W. (2002) *The Complete Kwanzaa: Celebrating our cultural harvest*. New York: Castle Books.

Ristock, J.L. (2002) *No More Secrets: Violence in lesbian relationships*. New York and London: Routledge.

Rogers, R. and Gallagher, K. (2006) 'African peoples' dance and the DARE project in Liverpool'. *Animated*, Spring. Online. www.communitydance.org.uk/DB/animated-library/african-peoples-dance-and-the-dare-project-in-live.html?ed=14046 (accessed 10 June 2015).

Roots Oral History Project (1992) *Rude Awakening: African Caribbean settlers in Manchester – An account*. Manchester: Roots Oral History Project.

The Runnymede Trust (1997) *Black and Ethnic Minority Young People and Educational Disadvantage*. Online. www.runnymedetrust.org/uploads/publications/pdfs/BMEYoungPeopleandEducationalDisadvantage-97.PDF (accessed 10 June 2015).

— (n.d.) *The Struggle for Racial Equality: An oral history of the Runnymede Trust, 1966–1988*. Online. www.runnymedetrust.org/histories/ (accessed 14 June 2014).

Russell, M. (1982) 'Black-Eyed Blues Connections: Teaching Black women'. In Hull, G.T., Scott. P.B. and Smith, B. (eds) *All the Women are White, All the Blacks are Men, But Some of Us are Brave: Black women's studies*. New York: Feminist Press, 196–207.

Russo, N.F. and Pirlott, A. (2006) 'Gender-based violence'. *Annals of the New York Academy of Sciences*, 1087 (1), 178–205.

Safety 4 Sisters Northwest (2010) 'Working towards securing greater protection, safety and support for women who have experienced gender violence and who have no recourse to public funds or state benefits'. Online. www.hssr.mmu.ac.uk/law-research/conference-securing-human-rights-for-women-from-abroad-experiencing-violence/ (accessed 10 June 2015).

Sallah, M. and Howson, C. (2007) *Working with Black Young People*. Lyme Regis: Russell House Publishing.

Scarman, L. (1981) *The Brixton Disorders, 10–12 April 1981*. London: HMSO.

Schaffe, T. (2009) 'Abasindi'. MA Television Documentary, University of Salford.

Schramm, K. (2007) 'Slave route projects: Tracing the heritage of slavery in Ghana'. In de Jong, F. and Rowlands, M. (eds). *Reclaiming Heritage: Alternative imaginaries of memory in West Africa*. Walnut Creek, CA: Left Coast Press, 71–98.

Selvon, S. (1956) *The Lonely Londoners*. London: Wingate.

Sewell, T. (1997) *Black Masculinities and Schooling: How Black boys survive modern schooling*. Stoke-on-Trent: Trentham Books.

Shepherd, V.A. (1999) *Women in Caribbean History*. Kingston: Ian Randle.

Shepherd, V., Brereton, B. and Bailey, R. (eds) (1995) *Engendering History: Caribbean women in historical perspective*. Kingston: Ian Randle.

Sherwood, M. (1999) *Claudia Jones: A life in exile: A biography*. London: Lawrence & Wishart.

Singh, A. and Webber, F. (2013) *Excluding Migrants from Justice: The legal aid cuts* (IRR Briefing Paper No. 7). Online. www.irr.org.uk/pdf2/IRR_Briefing_No.7.pdf (accessed 22 May 2015).

References

Sistren Theatre Collective and Ford-Smith, H. (1986) *Lionheart Gal: Life stories of Jamaican women*. London: The Women's Press.

Small, J. (1984) 'The crisis in adoption'. *International Journal of Social Psychiatry*, 30 (1–2), 129–42.

Sokoloff, N.J. and Dupont, I. (2005) 'Domestic violence at the intersections of race, class, and gender: Challenges and contributions to understanding violence against marginalized women in diverse communities'. *Violence Against Women*, 11 (1), 38–64.

Solomos, J. (2011) 'Race, rumours and riots: Past, present and future'. *Sociological Research Online*, 16 (4). www.socresonline.org.uk/16/4/20.html (accessed 22 May 2015).

Spellers, R.E. and Moffitt, K.R. (eds) (2010) *Blackberries and Redbones: Critical articulations of black hair/body politics in Africana communities*. New York: Hampton Press.

Sterling, L. (1995) 'Partners: The social organisations of rotating savings and credit societies among exilic Jamaicans'. *Sociology*, 29 (4), 653–66.

Stirling, S. (2009) *Public engagement fellowship conference report*. Manchester Conference for Black Parents, Children and Young People, 17 October..

Stone, M. (1981) *The Education of the Black Child in Britain: The myth of multiracial education*. London: Fontana Press.

Strand, S. and Winston, J. (2008) 'Educational aspirations in inner city schools'. *Eductional Studies*, 34 (4), 249–67.

Sudbury, J. (1998) *'Other Kinds of Dreams': Black women's organisations and the politics of transformation*. London and New York: Routledge.

Swaby, N. (2010) 'Amy Ashwood Garvey: A revolutionary Pan-African feminist'. Online. http://kalamu.posthaven.com/history-amy-ashwood-garvey-a-revolutionary-pa (accessed 22 May 2015).

Swann, Lord M. (1985) *Education for All: Final Report of the Committee of Inquiry into the Education of Children from Ethnic Minority Groups*. London: Her Majesty's Stationery Office.

Thiam, A. (1978) *Speak Out, Black Sisters: Feminism and oppression in Black Africa*. London: Pluto Press.

Thompson, C. (2009) 'Black women, beauty, and hair as a matter of *being*'. *Women's Studies*, 38 (8), 831–56.

Thomson, R., Bell, R., Holland, J., Henderson, S., McGrellis, S. and Sharpe, S. (2002) 'Critical moments: Choice, chance and opportunity in young people's narratives of transition'. *Sociology*, 36 (2), 335–54.

Trinh, T.M.-H. (1989) *Woman, Native, Other: Writing postcoloniality and feminism*. Bloomington: Indiana University Press.

Turner, R. (2011) '"Hope and despair" 30 years after the Moss Side riots'. BBC News, 8 July. Online. www.bbc.co.uk/news/uk-england-manchester-14047491 (accessed 10 June 2015).

Ung, T., O'Connor, S.H., Pillidge, R. (2012) 'The Development of Racial Identity in Transracially Adopted People – An Ecological Approach'. *Adoption & Fostering*, 38 (3–4), 73–84.

United Nations (1990) *Convention on the Rights of the Child*. Online. https://treaties.un.org/doc/publication/UNTS/Volume%201577/v1577.pdf (accessed 10 June 2015).

V&A (2015) 'History of Black Dance: Black British Dance'. Online. www.vam.ac.uk/content/articles/h/history-of-black-dance-black-british-dance/ (accessed 10 June 2015).

Voice for the Child in Care (2004) *The Care Experience: Through black eyes*. London: Voice for the Child in Care.

Wain, N. and Joyce, P. (2012) 'Disaffected communities, riots and policing: Manchester 1981 and 2011'. *Safer Communities*, 1 (3), 125–34.

Walker, A. (1983) *In Search of Our Mothers' Gardens: Womanist prose*. London: The Women's Press.

Washington, M.L. (1982) 'Teaching Black-Eyed Susans: An Approach to the Study of Black Women Writers'. In Hull, G.T., Scott, P.B. and Smith, B. (eds) *All the Women Are White, All the Blacks are Men, But Some of Us are Brave: Black Women's Studies*. New York: Feminist Press, 208–17.

Watt, D. (2002) 'Motherhood and mothering: The experience of three generations of Jamaican-heritage women in Manchester'. PhD thesis, Manchester Metropolitan University.

— (2013) 'Case study: Abasindi'. In Batsleer, J. *Youth Working with Girls and Women in Community Settings: A feminist perspective*. Farnham, Ashgate.

Webster, W. (1998) *Imagining Home: Gender, 'race' and national identity, 1945–64*. London: UCL Press.

Weekes, D. (1997) 'Shades of Blackness: Young Black female constructions of beauty'. In Mirza, H.S. (ed.) *Black British Feminism: A reader*. London: Taylor & Francis, 113–26.

Weiler, K. (2009) 'The history of women's education and the construction of the modern subject'. *Journal of Women's History*, 21 (2), 177–84.

Weiner, G. (1997) 'New era or old times: Class, gender and education'. Paper presented at the British Educational Research Association Annual Conference, University of York.

Welsh, K. (2004) *African Dance*. Chelsea: Chelsea House Publishers.

White, G. (1985) 'Black access to higher education'. In Pumfrey, P.D. and Verma, G.K. (eds) *Race relations and Urban Education: Contexts and promising practices*. Hove: Psychology Press.

Williams, F. (1997) 'Women and Community'. In Bornat, J., Pereira, C., Pilgrim, D. and Williams, F. (eds) *Community Care: A reader*. London: Macmillan, 33–42.

Willis, D. (ed.) (2010) *Black Venus 2010: They called her 'Hottentot'*. Philadelphia, PA: Temple University Press.

Wisker, G. (2000) *Post-Colonial and African American Women's Writing: A critical introduction*. London: Palgrave Macmillan.

'Women as role models' (1997) Conference report on an event celebrating the lives and achievements of Black women in Manchester.

Woodward, K. (1997) 'Introduction'. In Woodward, K (ed.) *Identity and Difference*. London: Sage in association with the Open University.

Wright, C., Standen, P. and Patel, T. (2010) *Black Youth Matters: Transitions from school to success*. New York and London: Routledge.

Zephaniah, B. (2005) 'Over and Out'. In Richardson, B. (ed.) *Tell It Like It Is: How our schools fail Black children*. Stoke-on-Trent: Bookmarks Publications, Trentham Books.

Index

Abasindi Drummers and Dancers 10, 58–84
Abbot, Diane 129
abortion 26
'absent father' phenomenon 147
access courses 152–7
achievement, concept of 31
activism 5, 7, 9, 11, 17, 20, 25–8, 39–41, 72–4, 80, 129, 162
Adichie, Chimamanda Ngozi 130
adoption of children 98
African Communities League 34
Africanness, sense of 41
'Afro' style 104
Alegi, Peter 45
Alexander, Z. 11
Ali, Mohammed 44
Ancestral Journey (dance drama) 65–8, 71–2
Andrews, Kehinde 129
Angelou, Maya 33
apartheid and the anti-apartheid movement 65, 77
art forms 9–10, 48–51, 54, 72, 128
Arts Council 51, 63
Ashe, F. 147, 149–50
assimilation 109–10
Asylum and Immigration Appeals Act (1993) 134
asylum seekers 97, 140–3
Ayesha 133–41

Baartman, Sarah 85–8, 91, 108
Badejo, Peter 72
Baldwin, James 146–7
Ballets Nègres 77
Bambata, Morenga 56
Banner, R. 66–8
Barbados 82–4
Barn, R. 98
Baxter, Carol 30
beauty, concepts and standards of 87–90, 104–8
Beck, Sharon 30
Beckford, G.L. 66
Beckles, Sir Hilary 33, 70–1
Bennett, Louise 112
Bennett, O. 53
Best, S. 68
Bhabha, J. 21
Black Sisters 28
Black studies programmes 153–4
Black womanhood 85–91, 104–5
Blackburn, F. 115, 117
Blackman, Roy 114
'Blackness', use of the term 93–4

Blake, Val 30
Bodey, Donald and Carol 145–6
body politics 86, 105
Brady, Cleveland 16
Brown, B. 106–7
Bryan, B. 11, 13, 30
Burman, E. 139

Cameroon 104
Campbell, B. 150
capitalism 107
career aspirations and careers services 123–9
Caribbean dance 76–7
Caribbean languages 111–12
Cariocca Enterprise 23, 120
Carmichael, Stokely 44
carnivals 7, 53, 78, 82
Carter, Trevor 110
Chakrabarti, M. 102
Cheng, A.A. 87–8, 90, 108
Chevannes, M. 109
children, treatment and involvement of 10, 60, 94–103, 106, 109–10, 118; *see also* education
Christian, Euston 16
City College Manchester Mentoring Programme 123
Clark, K.B. and M.K. 114
Clarke, J. 5
Coard, Bernard 10, 39–40, 110, 114
Cobham, R. 31
Collins, Merle 49–50
Collins, P.H. 5, 17, 26, 35, 129
Collins, S. 14
colonialism 42
Commission for Racial Equality (CRE) 30, 148, 154, 157
Commonwealth Immigration Act (1962) 7
'community', use of the term 13
council tenants 19
Craven, Judy 30
Creole languages 110
Critchlow, Charles 128
Crop Over Festival 82–3
Cross, W.E. 115–16
cultural capital 110, 126
cultural heritage 65, 76, 98, 115, 117
culture and cultural diversity 10, 138–9

Da-Cocodia, Louise 23–4, 30, 120–1, 162
Daily Mirror 6
DAISE model 115, 117, 121
Dalphinis, Morgan 111
dance: function and relevance of 63–5, 69, 71; politics of 72–8
Daniel, Alti 55–6
Davey, A. 114
Davis, E. 123–4
Deane, Wilma 30
Delado Dance and Drumming Group 48, 77
deprivation 144–5, 149

177

Dewjee, A. 11
discrimination 21–2, 33, 89, 106, 158
doll studies 114
domestic violence 136–9, 142, 150
Douglas, Ashton 16
Douglas, J.D. 5–6
Dow, George 43
Du Bois, W.E.B. 79–80
Duggan, Mark 148–9
Duncan, Melanie 15
Dupont, I. 138–9
Dzikunu, George 72

education 10, 19, 26, 39–40, 109–29, 132, 142–3, 146, 148, 152–7, 161–3
Edwards, Beresford 110
Edwards, Christine 118–19
Edwards, Elouise 25–6, 30, 53, 55, 114, 121, 151
Edwards-Kerr, D. 129
Ekejuiba, A.F. 14
Elmina Castle 80–1
Emery, Lynne Fauley 71
Empire Windrush 14–16
employment patterns 17–21, 24–6
Engels, Friedrich 16
'Enlightenment' discourse 67
extended families 14

Fanon, F. 41, 44
Farrar, M. 13
femininity, Black 91–2
feminism and feminist scholarship 10, 27, 35–7, 72, 87, 89, 105, 130–1
Finiken, Lana 49
Ford-Smith, Honor 35, 49
Freire, Paulo 40–1
Frost, D. 148
Fryer, P. 14–15

Garvey, Amy Ashwood 11, 16–17
Garvey, Amy Jacques 9, 11, 17, 34–5
Garvey, Marcus 16–17, 35–6, 44
Garvey movement 35
Gates, Henry Jr 67
genealogical research 47
Ghana 78–84; National Dance Company 81–2
Gilchrist, E.S. 86
Glass, R. 14
Glean, Beverley 77
Gordon, Shirley 57
Gore, Pip 16
Gramsci, A. 130
Grannum, Guy 47
Greater Manchester Immigration Aid Unit 141
Greater Manchester Police 40
Grimes, M.D. 136
Griot-historians 5

hair and hairstyles 10, 88, 104–7, 159
Hall, Stuart 138
Haraway, Donna 85–7, 91, 105
Hetty 66–9, 72
Hill, M. 102
Hill Collins, P. 94, 106
Hinds, Donald 7
Hoare, Q. 130
Holmes, R. 87–8
home ownership 18–19
hooks, bell 104, 113, 125
housing 18–19, 39
Hulme 16–19, 26, 40
Humphreys, C. 138
Hurston, Zora Neale 34
hybridization of dance forms 76

identity, sense of 95–6, 114–15
identity formation 10
immigration status and controls 134, 139–42
Innis, Shirley 177
Institute of Race Relations 141
intersectional analysis 140, 150
Irie Dance Theatre 77
Irish immigrants 6

Jackson, R.L. 86
Jamaican Business Women's Association 36
Jamaican National Dance Company 65
Jamaican Patois 112–13, 161
Jarrett-Macauley, D. 36
Javed, H.M. 109, 124–6
Jefferson, Thomas 87
Jones, Adele D. 158–9; *co-author*
Jones, Claudia 6–7

Kankpeyeng, B.W. 80
Kant, Immanuel 87
Kantamanto Drumming Group 48
Karenga, Maulena 51, 84
Karn, V. 18
Kath Locke Centre 78
Kenyatta, Jomo 41, 45
Kerr, Edwards 121, 123
King, D.K. 34
King, Martin Luther 13
Kirton, D. 98
Kirwen, M.C. 45
Krio language 160–1
Kwanzaa 51–2, 78, 84

Lancaster, Judy 55
languages 111–12, 160–1
Larrabee, M.J. 72
Lawford, Aubery 16
Lawrence, D. 6
Lawrence, Stephen 162
LaYacona, M. 65
legal representation and legal aid 141–2

lesbianism 27
Lewis, Arthur 40
Lewis, G. 11, 20
Likoya, Abina 48, 55, 59–63, 77, 82
local authority care for children 95–9, 102
Locke, Kath 7–9, 20, 28–30, 37–41, 65
Lorde, Audre 1
Louise Da-Cocodia Educational Trust 10, 109, 120–3
Lovejoy, P. 87
Luckham, Betty 121

Maathai, Wangari 111–12
McDonald, Brenda 125
McKenzie, Victoria 112–13, 161
Macpherson Report (1999) 152–3
Majors, Richard 124
Makeba, Miriam 44
Making Education a Priority – Alternative Approaches conference (2013) 129
Makonnen, Ras 38, 41
Malcolm X 44
Mama, Amina 139–40
Manchester 15–17, 20, 25, 39–40
Manchester Black Access Course 10, 154–7
Manchester Black Parents, Children and Young People Conference (2009) 127–8
Manchester Black Women's Cooperative 25–6, 132
Manchester Black Women's Mutual Aid 24, 29
Manchester City Council 19, 39, 56
Mandela, Nelson 45, 65, 77, 86
Mandela, Winnie 65
Mann, S.A. 136
Manning, Edward 43
Marco, J.L. 106
Marcus, S. 68
Maroons 33, 77
Marson, Una 9, 11, 21, 36–7
Matthews, M.D. 35
Maxime, J. 114–15
May, Shirley 7–8, 164
Mayne, Liz 56
men's involvement with Abasindi Cooperative 5, 130
Mercer, K. 105
Messado, Francia 12–13, 108
Messerschmidt, J.W. 150
Milburn, K. 149
Miller, Prince 54
Milliard, Peter 16
Mirza, H. 129
Monday Club 148
Morokvasic, M. 6
Morris, Olive 37
Morrison, Toni 95–6, 160
mortgages 18

Moss Side 17–20, 26, 38–40, 50–2, 143, 161; 1981 disturbances in 10, 40, 51, 110, 143–7, 150–1
Moss Side Arts Group (MAG) 5, 48, 51, 55
Moss Side Defence Committee 150–1
Moss Side and Hulme Women's Action Forum 29–30
Moss Side People's Centre 1, 19
mother tongues 111–12

naming/renaming as an aspect of identity 43–6
Nanny of the Maroons 33
National Health Service 21, 24, 30
National Union of Students 152
Negro Factories Corporation 34
The Negro World (newspaper) 35
Nelson, Tom 16
neoliberalism 149
Nettleford, R.M. 65
Nia Cultural Centre 9–10, 47–8, 51–2, 55–7
Nigeria 137
Nightingale, Florence 24
'Nigresence' model 115
Nii-Yartey, F. 82
Nixon, J. 138
Nkrumah, Kwame 44, 79, 82
Noble, Maria 26–9
North West Arts Board 56
Notting Hill Carnival 7
nursing 21–3
Nyamnjoh, F.B. 104–5, 107

Obadina, T. 79
Odueso, Thomas 58–9
Okojie, Paul 37–8
Okuboh, Ervine 55
Omalade, B. 5
oral history 11
Organization for Women of Asian and African Descent 25, 28
owner-occupiers 18–19

Pan-African Congress (Manchester, 1945) 15–16, 28, 35, 38, 41, 79–80
Pan-African Congress (Paris, 1919) 79
Pan-African Congress (Tanzania, 1974) 35
Pan-Africanism 79–80, 130
PANAFEST festival 78–81
Parham, T.A. 115
Pedraza, S. 6
performative agency 68–9
Phillips, Mike 15
Phillips, R. 16–17, 148
Phillips, Trevor 15
Phinney, J.S. 115, 117
Phoenix Dance Company 77
Pilkington, E. 71
Platts-Fowler, D. 149

Plowden Report (1967)   110
policing   40, 143–51, 162
Polish immigrants   6
political engagement   25, 39, 63, 72–8, 130
politicization   10, 152, 154
Pollins, H.   14
poverty   140, 142
Prince, Mary   66–9, 72
Pringle, Thomas   68
Proctor, Harvey   148
Pryce, K.   6

QPH (play)   50

racism   10, 20, 28, 30, 33, 38, 40, 65, 78, 85, 89–90, 96, 99–106, 109, 115–17, 126, 130, 139, 142–4, 147–9, 152, 158–9, 162–3; acquiescence with   106; institutional   101, 110, 152–3, 158; internalized   102, 106
Ramdhanie, B.   66, 74, 76, 78
Rampton Committee   110
REACH Report (2007)   123
Reeves, F.   109
religion   41–3, 75, 131
'rememorying'   80
Renkin, Jules   42–3
reparations for slavery and the slave trade   69–70
repatriation of immigrants   148
residence patterns   18–19
resilience   33–4
Rex, John   145–6
Richie, B.E.   136
Riley, D.W.   33, 52
rioting: in 1981   148–9, 152–3; in 2011   148–9; *see also* Moss Side: 1981 disturbances in
Robinson, Gil   153
role models   123
Roots Festival   10, 24–5, 28, 53
Runnymede Trust   124
Russell, William Howard   24

Safety 4 Sisters Northwest   142
Sankofa, Olajumoke   46
Saturday supplementary school   10, 109, 113–23, 127–9, 161–2
scholarship: separation from activism   5; *see also* feminism and feminist scholarship
Schramm, K.   70
Seacole, Mary   11, 24–5
Sekou Touré, Ahmed   44
self, sense of   116
self-improvement and self-empowerment   39
Selvon, Sam   6
Sewell, T.   126
sexism   20, 27, 30
sexual division of labour   20

sexuality   6, 86–7
Shakespeare, William   160
Shakur, Assata Olugba   45
Shange, Ntozake   44
Shutter, S.   21
Sierra Leone   159–60
Simone, Nina   56
Singh, A.   141–2
single-parent households   126, 147, 149
sisterhood, politics of   130
Sistren Theatre Collective   37, 49–50
slave trade, trans-Atlantic   70–2, 76, 80
slavery   13–14, 16, 20, 43, 47, 64–71, 76–7, 83–4; abolition of   67, 71; in British society   71; in West Africa   70
slaves' autobiographies   67–8
Small, J.   96
Smith, Leon   16
social capital   41, 113, 126, 162
Sokoloff, N.J.   138–9
souls   41–2
Stephen Lawrence Charitable Trust   162
stereotyping, institutional   122
Sterling, L.   18
Stone, Maureen   111
'stop and search' powers   143, 145, 149–50
storytelling as an art form   128
Strand, S.   126–7
Strategy to Elevate People (STEP)   123
SuAndi   4, 33, 64, 83, 89, 152, 161
Sudbury, J.   25
Sumner, Phil   145
Swann Report (1985)   110, 153
Sweeney, Linford   48

Tafary, Levi   48
Teacher Empathy programme   124–5
Thatcher, Margaret   142–3, 148, 157
Thiam, Awa   56
Thompson, C.   86, 105
Thomson, R.   126
traditional African dance (TAD)   74–7
Trafford Park industrial complex   17
transracial adoption/fostering   98
traveller communities   140
Trinh Minh-ha   91–2
Truth, Sojourner   34, 85, 90–1, 96, 108

UK Border Agency   140
under-achievement   121
unemployment   143, 149
unions   21
United Nations Convention on the Rights of the Child   126
United Nations Educational, Scientific and Cultural Organization (UNESCO)   80
Universal Negro Improvement Association (UNIA)   16, 34–5

Index

Voice for the Child in Care   102
voodoo   42–3

Walker, Alice   11, 34, 39, 47, 57
Watt, D.   22, 53, 111, 158–9;   *co-author*
Webber, F.   141–2
welfare support   134, 136, 140–2, 147–9
Werbner, Pnina   54–5
The West Indian Gazette   6–7
West Indian Overseas
    Coordinating Committee   10, 23, 53
West Indian Sports and Social
    Club, Moss Side   16
'White flight'   38
Williams, Henry Sylvester   79

Winston, J.   126–7
women's liberation   80
women's rights   90, 142
Woodward, K.   43
Wright, C.   126
Wythenshawe   116

Yinka   92–4
YouTube   107

Zephaniah, Benjamin   122–3
Zion Arts Centre   128
Zulu war dances   72–3

Our last thoughts are for Shirley Innis, a beautiful spirit and one of the founder members of Abasindi.